Marriage: From Surviving to Thriving

Marriage: From Surviving to Thriving

Practical Advice on Making Your Marriage Strong

CHARLES R. SWINDOLL

W PUBLISHING GROUP
A Division of Thomas Nelson Publishers
Since 1798

www.wpublishinggroup.com

MARRIAGE: FROM SURVIVING TO THRIVING

Copyright © 2006, Charles R. Swindoll.

Published by W Publishing Group, a Division of Thomas Nelson, Inc., P.O. Box 141000, Nashville, TN, 37214.

W Publishing Group books may be purchased in bulk for educational, business, fundraising, or sales promotional use. For information, please email SpecialMarkets@ThomasNelson.com.

All Scripture quotations, unless otherwise indicated, are taken from New American Standard Bible. Copyright © 1960, 1962, 1963, 1968, 1971, 1973, 1975, 1977, 1995 by The Lockman Foundation, La Habra, California. Used by permission.

Other Scripture references are from the following sources:

The NET Bible® (NET) copyright © 2003 by Biblical Studies Press, L.L.C. www.netbible.com All rights reserved. Used by permission.

The Message (MSG) by Eugene Peterson. Copyright © 1993, 1994, 1995, 1996, 2000, 2001, 2002. Used by permission of NavPress Publishing Group. All rights reserved.

Editorial Staff: Shady Oaks Studio, 1507 Shirley Way, Bedford, TX 76022.

Cover Design: TOBIAS' OUTERWEAR FOR BOOKS
Page Design: Inside Out Design & Typesetting, Fort Worth, TX

Published in association with Yates and Yates, LLP, Attorneys and Counselors, Orange, California.

Library of Congress Cataloging-in-Publication Data

Swindoll, Charles R.
    Marriage: from surviving to thriving : practical advice on making your marriage strong / Charles R. Swindoll.
       p.   cm.
       Summary: "Practical applications to help a marriage go from surviving to thriving"—Provided by publisher.
    Includes bibliographical references and index.
    ISBN 0-8499-0150-2 (hardcover : alk. paper)
    1. Marriage—Religious aspects—Christianity.   I. Title.
    BV835.S93   2006
    248.8'44—dc22   2006011499

Printed in the United States of America
06 07 08 09 10   QW   9 8 7 6 5 4 3 2 1

This is for you, Cynthia.

After more than fifty years of
our being on this journey together,
sharing equally in the sorrows and struggles,
as well as in the accomplishments and pleasures,
my commitment to you is stronger than ever,
my respect for you is greater than ever,
and my love for you is deeper than ever.

Contents

Acknowledgments

---⚭---

Any marriage that has lasted as long as ours includes others—many others—who have played significant roles in both our lives. First, Cynthia and I have our parents, Leslie and Laverne Parker and Earl and Lovell Swindoll, to thank for their long-term marriages. As we were reared in our original homes, we observed the things they modeled that held them together. To this day my wife and I often recall many of those qualities and acknowledge what a powerful influence they had on each of us. How grateful we are for our faithful parents—all four now with the Lord.

In addition, there has been the influence of our now-adult children and their marriages. We've learned numerous lessons and received very helpful insights from all four of them and their relationships with their marriage partners. Our love for each one knows no bounds.

And then there have been teachers, mentors, colleagues, and all our wonderful friends who have contributed so much over these years . . . too many to mention. Their encouragement and belief in us have, in many ways, helped us stay at it, as we've endured days that were borderline unbearable and as we've enjoyed and celebrated far more that were delightful and fun.

When I decided to write this book, I have my publisher, David Moberg of W Publishing Group, to thank for his strong encouragement, as well as Mark Gaither, my son-in-law, for his excellent editorial skills and assistance. And I must acknowledge Mary Hollingsworth and her fine staff at Shady Oaks Studio in Fort Worth for putting the finishing touches on this volume, making it both attractive and presentable.

Finally, to my bride of fifty-one years, the mother of our children, my faithful and devoted partner in ministry, the one who knows me and understands me, and still loves me more than anyone else on the planet—what more can I say?

My heartfelt thanks to all!

Introduction

$\mathcal{O}$n June 18, 1955, two very young people were married. He had just turned twenty; she was only eighteen.

Only seven days after their first date, he was convinced that she was "the woman of his dreams," so he asked her to marry him. Though only sixteen at the time and still in the eleventh grade of high school, the teenage girl said yes. A little over eighteen months later, they married and began their journey that would last for more than five decades. And what a journey it has been! Four married children, currently from their midthirties to their midforties, and ten grandchildren who range in age from a second-grader to a recent college graduate now comprise their family.

Who would have ever guessed, way back in the mid-1950s, that so much would have happened to them and among them . . . and who could have ever imagined all the lives they would touch and all the amazing things they would experience as those fifty-plus years ran their course? The fact that those two have remained together is the most amazing part of all—only because of God's grace!

By now you've guessed that my wife and I are that original couple.

Looking back over these many years of marriage, as we do every now and then, Cynthia and I often sigh and sometimes smile. Contrary to popular opinion, we've not been sheltered from life's harsh winds. To make matters even more challenging, neither of us has been all that easy to live with. Truth be told, our marriage has literally spanned the extremes: from surviving to thriving. But the good news is, we've made it this far! Much of that is because we've found some of the things that make a marriage work, and we've applied them as often as possible.

It occurred to me that some of those things we learned are worth passing along; hence this little book. If it helps, I'm grateful. Please share what you read with others. If it doesn't, I'm sorry. Please keep that to yourself. I'd hate to think I made a weak marriage worse.

—CHUCK SWINDOLL
Frisco, Texas

One

This Is Not Your Grandfather's Family

⚭

*I*magine for a few moments that you are a modern-day Rip van Winkle. You're enjoying a relatively normal life in the mid-1960s with a mate at your side and children under the age of ten living at home. Life is good, yet a subtle uneasiness occasionally disturbs your peace. After the turmoil of Kennedy's assassination, Washington has returned to its usual bickering with Lyndon Johnson as the thirty-sixth president of the United States. All's quiet in Cuba and the Soviet Union for the moment, but that troublesome skirmish in Southeast Asia seems to be escalating.

You're also concerned because your children are now listening to the Beach Boys after a man known simply as Elvis introduced a different kind of music to popular audiences. His swiveling hips and suggestive antics have robbed television of its earlier innocence, but you patiently endure the Smothers Brothers and are learning to tolerate the edgy, off-color humor on *Laugh-In*. After all, there's always Lawrence Welk on Saturday night and *Bonanza* every Sunday evening after church.

"Weed" is what keeps your flowers from blooming larger, "pot" is where you grow herbs, a "mouse" is a pesky rodent, Coke is a soft drink, and "gay" means you're happy. *Abortion, incest, homosexuality,* and *condom* are words you would never hear from a pulpit and rarely in public. Beatniks have become hippies, but you never see them anywhere except on television, usually living in communes or somewhere between Santa Cruz and Portland, or maybe out on Cape Cod at the opposite coast.

For the most part, you enjoy your home and your quiet neighborhood. It's a safe place to be. Your kids take off on their bikes each Saturday morning, and except for lunch, you don't see them again until dark. You don't worry because the other parents help keep an eye out for trouble, rare as it is.

Life is good. Not perfect, but good. Simple. Stable. Manageable. Then . . . you lie down for a nap.

When you open your eyes, forty years have gone by. Your children are now in their forties and your mate is gone. Having decided you would probably never meet his or her personal needs, divorce seemed the only reasonable alternative to ensure long-term happiness. And so your spouse has found another. Your homestead has been replaced by high-rise apartments, and affluence has displaced the simplicity and security of your old neighborhood. You're interested in exploring the world that has covered over the green, landscaped patches that surrounded your little yard. But you frown, realizing it's not safe out there anymore.

Staying in doesn't feel much better. A contraption in your study has pornography on it, so you stay out of there. Your television has ten times the channels it used to and four-letter words pepper most of the programs, including newscasts, sports shows, and especially late-night talk shows. You used to roll your eyes because married couples on television slept in twin beds, but now characters go through multiple partners in a single episode. In fact, you can see most of the between-the-sheets details on any given weekday afternoon.

In the world beyond your neighborhood, prayer is increasingly illegal while abortion is encouraged. Churches in mainline denominations are performing more and more same-sex marriage ceremonies. Voice your objections on biblical grounds, and immediately you will find yourself accused of "hate speech" and labeled "homophobic."

Children are fed raw sexuality and brutal violence while sociologists marvel at the rise of bloodshed and teenage sex at school. Society's solution: pass them through metal detectors and hand them a condom.

To say that things have changed is a gross understatement.

In the late 1960s, Dallas Theological Seminary hosted a three-day lectureship featuring Dr. Francis Schaeffer. I sat spellbound as this unusual, modern-day prophet wearing a turtleneck sweater and knickers painted a vivid picture of our times. He revealed patterns in art and literature as they progressed through history, leading up to where we were then. He even ventured a few shocking predictions that have since come to pass. The exact words of his last prediction have never left my mind: "Someday we will wake up and find that the America we once knew is gone." Schaeffer, though dead now, still speaks. How right he was!

THIS IS NOT YOUR GRANDFATHER'S FAMILY

The effect on the family has not been a small one. The images of domestic roles have become so smeared, we can barely recognize them. A masculine father who carries out his role as the spiritual leader of the family must do so apologetically. However tender and sensitive his approach, our culture will accuse him of being patriarchal and authoritarian. A feminine mother who delights in her role as caregiver and supporter will disappoint a watching world. Despite her dignified, sacrificial strength, too many will leave her with the odd feeling that she has something to prove. Besides, in this culture of blurred lines, the children have become the centerpiece of the home. Everything must revolve around their wants and needs. However, even today as you look at homes where the children are happiest, you'll see that their well-being grows out of an enduring, intimate union between their mom and dad. That hasn't changed even a little.

But then I can hardly blame the "children-first" reformers. Let's face facts. For many, the home is no longer a safe place. James Patterson and Peter Kim, authors of *The Day America Told the Truth*, are undeniably correct when they say that America is the most violent country in the world, and that the home is the epicenter of that violence. Stories of spouse abuse and child abuse have become so common that we have lost our sense of outrage.

Men afraid to be men. Women ashamed of being women. Children unsure of who's in charge. Homes that have become battlegrounds. And all of it so unstable, so temporary. In some respects, admittedly, things are better than forty years ago, but in so many others, far worse. We can debate each point endlessly, but we must agree on one inescapable truth: this is not your grandfather's family.

A Helpful Perspective

Let me assure you at this point that this chapter isn't heading where you might expect, so bear with me. Conservative politicians often begin their speeches much the way I have chosen to lead off this book. They spout statistics and point to alarming downward trends in order to grab the attention of fearful constituents and then promise a political solution. I support many of them and hope they contribute a positive influence in whatever office they hold. Still other social reformers decry the evils of modern technology and its threat to families. My message is pointed and direct, but it's not meant to sound cranky or old-fashioned. I have no interest in returning to yesteryear. I love the conveniences and delights of today's time. I wouldn't go back if I could.

I write this, not as a politician and not as a social scientist, but as a husband, a dad, a granddad, a pastor, and hopefully, your friend. My desire is to have everyone reading these pages, whether young or old, conservative or liberal, optimistic or pessimistic, begin this straightforward look at marriage and family from the same vantage point, with this simple axiom:

**The world has changed,
and it's going to keep changing.**

That's no big revelation, I realize, but keeping it in the forefront of our minds will help us in three important ways. First, it tears from our clutching fingers the futile and frustrating hope that we can ever return to the past. Second, it alerts us to the fact that *we* are changing as things around us change. Third, it urges us to look for something permanent.

Face the Future

We can't solve modern problems by going back in time. Retreating to the safety of the familiar is an understandable response, but God has called us to a life of faith. And faith requires us to face the unknown while trusting Him completely. Furthermore, clinging to the good ol' days prevents older generations from teaching younger ones. Young families need perspective and encouragement to help them deal with today, where decisions shape the future—a future we will all share.

Examine Yourself

I have experienced, as I'm sure you have, a change in my thinking as our society has changed. When we first encounter extreme evil, we naturally react with shock and outrage. I remember the chill that ran down my spine when I read of the mother who drowned her children by running her car into a lake. I was outraged by the mother who drowned her children in a bathtub. Then as a few more of these stories came to light, I noticed that each time I was a little more detached than the last. I felt myself move from shock to detachment, to indifference, to apathy. In unguarded moments, I must confess to a gradual, inevitable slide toward a passive acceptance of what I know to be wrong. What once made me blush now saddens me but rarely shocks me.

I wish I could say I'm still surprised to hear of believers living together without a marriage covenant. I don't accept it. I won't condone it. Our church must take disciplinary action if this situation involves our members, but I'm not as disturbed as I once was. My biblical stand remains as firm as ever on the matter, but no thanks to a culture that has moved from apathy to full acceptance of this sin and so many others.

A few, very influential leaders in popular culture use this slippery slope to advance their personal agenda. In a 1991 interview with *The Advocate*, a homosexual publication, entertainer Madonna answered a pointed question about the provacative images she used in her videos and her stage act, and what effect they might have on teenage kids in Middle America. In response, she said kids digest the unusual, gender-confused images on a number of levels. She expected that some would be consciously disgusted, yet unconsciously aroused and challenged by the sight of men dancing with one another in women's lingerie. Others might be amused by the irony, which will help them overcome their fear of the forbidden. She concluded her statement by suggesting that, by repeated exposure, the provocative would gradually become less bizarre, more normal.

Don't be fooled. This is more than harmless fun or mere "artistic expression." This is a conscious effort to move our moral boundaries by degrees.[1]

Pause, and let that sink in.

Robert Lewis, a pastor in Little Rock, Arkansas, wrote these very astute words in his book, *Real Family Values*:

> The Christian family looks on while people in authority make decisions that contradict everything they know to be true. . . .
>
> Anesthetized by a corrupt culture, many families have lost the ability to discern between good and evil. Our moral edge has become dull. Our children sit next to us on the sofa at night soaking up the opinions,

values, and images of a godless society. Our silence and passivity are lethal to them. And then we have the audacity to marvel at their lack of spiritual passion and their propensity for moral compromise![2]

If you're like most believers, it's very possible that your conscience has been desensitized. Perhaps you sometimes find yourself rethinking some truths that you know are in the Scriptures but wonder now if they're relevant. Beware! You're feeling the tug of gravity, and a helpless slide into moral compromise is not far away. Trust me, I've felt it. No one is immune.

Search for Truth

With all of this talk of change, we need to focus our attention on some unchanging truths—things that haven't changed.

First, *the heart of humanity hasn't changed.* You and I are, by birth, by nature, and by choice, inwardly depraved, which is to say that we are entirely corrupt. That's not to say that we have no good in us; we do. However, anything good in us has been tainted with evil. It touches everything. Without the redeeming power of Christ we cannot halt our own moral slide. Only the power of the Holy Spirit working within us can do that.

Second, *God's desire for His people hasn't changed.* God is holy and just and pure. He tells us in the Scriptures to be as He is, so He expects His people to be holy, just, and pure. Not prudish, not dated, not cranky, but holy and just and pure. We know this is possible, because He would never give us a directive that cannot be fulfilled. Furthermore, He promised those who are His that He would transform us by His power. This has not changed. We can count on it.

Third, *God continues to be faithful and compassionate, and He wants us to be faithful and compassionate.* We can stand against what is clearly wrong and definitely contrary to the Scriptures and, with no sense of conflict, love those who live another way. Yes, we can proclaim the truth of God's Word while reaching out in genuine interest to improve the lives of others. In fact, that was the essence of Christ's ministry on earth. But don't expect any medals. Just as Jesus was crucified, so you can expect a cool response at best and outright persecution at worst. But know that if you do it correctly, lives will be impacted for Him. God's holiness hasn't changed; neither has His compassion.

Fourth, *God's truth remains unchanged, as revealed in the Scriptures.* As the popular media challenges traditional concepts and desensitizes our moral nerve endings, and as the courts redefine truth to accommodate an evolving moral standard, we can count on the Bible to reflect the mind of God, who is the source of all truth. All else may fail, but, as always, we can count on God's Word.

Let me summarize everything I have said so far:

**The world has changed
and it's going to keep changing,
but God never changes;
so we are safe when we cling to Him.**

HOPE FOR THE FAMILY IN GENERAL AND YOUR MARRIAGE IN PARTICULAR

Our goal in this book is not to recover a bygone era but to remain current and relevant without compromising our commitment to the truth of God's Word. The statement above was no less true when Moses wrote Deuteronomy than it is today. Change is not new. Certainly, things change from generation to generation, but even within a generation, nothing remains the same. Look back over the years you spent in your family of origin. Didn't it seem as though your parents were always coping with one big change or another? The new addition to the family or surprising death. The different job. The unfamiliar location. The different house or school or car or level of income. As

I say in my book, *Getting Through the Tough Stuff,* it's **always something!**

The events recorded in Deuteronomy occurred after a lot of changes. And the people of Israel were about to face even more. Jacob's sons had settled in Egypt as a great famine ravaged Canaan, the Promised Land. But as Canaan recovered, the Hebrew people remained in a very prosperous region of Egypt. As is often the case, prosperity eroded into slavery, and the Israelites couldn't leave if they wanted to. After 430 years in Egypt, God delivered them from their bondage, giving them Moses as their leader. Talk about changes!

Moses led this nation of perhaps as many as two million people out of Egypt to reclaim the land that God had given them through their forefather, Abraham. But when they arrived at the border and sized up the competition, the Israelites failed to trust the Lord. They voted to return to slavery rather than conquer the land He had promised to give them. To punish the unbelieving generation, He caused the nation to live as nomads until their children were old enough to carry on. Megachanges accompanied those difficult decades.

After forty years of wandering, the nation was finally ready to enter the land. Moses, at 120 years of age, had come to the end of his life. Deuteronomy represents his last word to the people of Israel. Like a venerable great-grandfather on his deathbed, Moses pulled his family around him and reiterated his most important lessons. That's where we get the name of the book. *Deutero* means "second." *Nomos* means "law." Deuteronomy is the retelling of the Law of God in practical terms.

Moses also understood this to be a pivotal moment in Israel's life as a nation. They would move into cities that they didn't establish and live in houses they didn't build. They would eat from trees and vines they didn't plant and drink from wells they didn't dig. The people of God would enjoy a lifestyle with such wealth and prosperity that the danger of forgetting their God loomed large. His words began with a simple truth:

> Hear, O Israel! The LORD is our God, the LORD is one! (Deuteronomy 6:4)

This begins a passage the Jewish people call the *shema*, (pronounced "she-MAH"). The name comes from the first word out of Moses's mouth, which means "hear," and it's a command. Listen! Listen to this fundamental truth: God is your master, and He is your only master. He is absolutely unique and no other God exists. And this fundamental truth naturally leads to the most important commandment.

> You shall love the LORD your God with all your heart
> and with all your soul and with all your might.
> (Deuteronomy 6:5)

In other words, "Hold nothing back. Love Him with everything you are and with everything you have." This truth and this commandment were to bind each individual in a personal relationship with God. Furthermore, each was to pass it on to his or her mate and family members by letting this truth permeate every aspect of life.

> You shall teach them diligently to your sons and shall
> talk of them when you sit in your house and when
> you walk by the way and when you lie down and
> when you rise up. (Deuteronomy 6:7)

The word translated "teach" is from a Hebrew word that means "sharpen" in the literal sense and "repeat" in the figurative. When sharpening a blade with a stone, the metal is scraped repeatedly until its edge is sharp. The verb is an intensive form, suggesting "teach your children this truth *continually* by talking about it and living it out in front of them." This is more than family devotions and a memorized prayer over dinner. A passionate devotion to God was to permeate every aspect of the home, starting with the married couple and then, as children came, the parents. Verse 10 explains why Moses taught this with such passionate zeal.

> When the LORD your God brings you into the land which He swore to your fathers, Abraham, Isaac and Jacob, to give you, great and splendid cities which you did not build, and houses full of all good things which you did not fill, and hewn cisterns which you did not dig, vineyards and olive trees which you did not plant, and you eat and are satisfied, then watch yourself, that you do not forget the LORD who brought you from the land of Egypt, out of the house of slavery. . . . So the LORD commanded us to observe all these statutes, to fear the LORD our God *for our good always and for our survival*, as it is today. (Deuteronomy 6:10–12, 24; emphasis added)

Moses had been a visible sign of God's presence during Israel's exodus from Egypt and during forty years of nomadic life in the wilderness. As a prophet, he was the Lord's mouthpiece. He delivered God's statutes. He led the Hebrews in battle. He organized their religious practice. He established their government. Like a father, he interceded for them, taught them, chastised them, and nurtured them in their relationship with the Lord. He had seen them through many changes. Now, like a parent releasing a child into the world, Moses wanted them to stand on their own—to personally own the Law of God. In essence, he said, "I am passing away, but these laws remain. Remember this: they are *for your good* and they are necessary *for your survival*. Ignore them to your own peril! If that occurs, you will absorb the pagan cultures and lifestyle of the Canaanites like a dry sponge. You will be extinct within a generation."

So it is with us. Jesus superseded the Law of Moses. We no longer approach God through a system of statutes and temple sacrifices. However, the principles of His Word are no less important and the imperative no less passionate. When an expert in the Law of Moses asked Jesus which commandment was the greatest, Jesus answered,

> The foremost is, "Hear, O Israel! The Lord our God is one Lord; and you shall love the Lord your God with all your heart, and with all your soul, and with all your mind, and with all your strength." (Mark 12:29–30)

In an ever-changing world, this remains permanent. As we feel the tug of gravity pulling us toward an inescapable moral slide, we can cling to this. Our relationship with the Lord is not only good, it is essential for our survival. Your marriage and your family are still the very best ways to ensure the good and survival of future generations.

FOUR STRONG PRINCIPLES
AND NO-NONSENSE APPLICATIONS

All of this leads me to some principles that are both true and timeless. They will also prepare us for the chapters to come. Think first of your *marriage* and then your *family*.

Wake Up!

Complacency blinds us to reality. As we drift with the current of our culture, following the path of least resistance, we fail to notice the growing distance between us and the Lord. How easy it is to trivialize wrong, become indifferent to it, tolerate it, accept it, and finally embrace it. Wake up! Look at where you are in relation to the Lord and determine to focus on it realistically.

This is no time for a nap. If it's just you and your marriage partner, stay awake and alert to the subtle pleadings of compromises. If you have small children living with you, be proactive in discovering how their culture might be influencing them. If you have teenagers, invest some time watching the television shows they watch and listening to the music they enjoy. You may have to intervene, but better if you understand the messages they are receiving so that the world isn't the only voice your children hear.

Don't be fooled by their nonchalance. You can't silence the world, but then you don't have to. Your children are eager for direction in the midst of what is for them a time of confusion and change. They only pretend to disregard your advice and your involvement. In fact, your word counts far more than they are willing to admit. They may shrug and roll their eyes, but they're hearing you.

Listen Up!

Knowledge sets us free. The enemy of our soul preys on ignorance. As long as Satan, the ruler of this world, can keep you in ignorance, he can delude you with superstition and fear. He'll twist your theology in order to keep you chasing the wrong solutions. The consequences of that drift are devastating! Your spiritual life will be dominated by uncertainties and insecurities. You'll find yourself confused about who you are and where you're going.

Jesus said this about being His disciple: "If you continue in My word, then you are truly disciples of Mine; and you will know the truth, and the truth will make you free" (John 8:31–32). When you are growing in your *knowledge* of God's Word, that equips you to think clearly and see the world realistically. Study Scripture. Read it daily. Memorize key passages. Whenever I dedicate myself to that exercise, I am amazed by how my discernment is sharpened—how much better I handle life's routine trials.

Step Up!

We need to be like the men of Issachar. The Bible says of them, "From Issachar there were 200 leaders and all their relatives at their command—*they understood the times and knew what Israel should do*" (1 Chronicles 12:32 NET; emphasis added).

A keen understanding of our culture prompts us to act courageously. When we can see things as God sees them, and as we survey the world with God's perspective, we find within ourselves a kind of God-prompted, supernatural courage to take a stand, to be different. It takes wisdom to do that without appearing either pathetic or condemning. While we want our difference to be attractive, we will nonetheless experience rejection and ridicule. Still we must act.

Give support to those men and women in public office you know to be Christians. Get behind legislation that protects traditional marriage and the family as God structured them originally. Fight anything that would drag our society away from the scriptural principles that God gave us for our good and for our survival. Think of yourself as a modern-day son or daughter of Issachar.

Look Up!

God loves us unconditionally. That's good news we need to remember often. As you read this book, struggles in your marriage and/or your family may be causing great sorrow, fear, or doubt. Perhaps the tension in your marriage threatens to tear it apart. Or maybe pressures from the outside have disrupted your relationship and made intimacy more of a challenge. You may have made poor or even tragic decisions that have put your marriage in jeopardy. Whatever your situation, whatever challenge you face, God loves you unconditionally, and He wants your marriage not only to survive but to thrive. Look up! Call on Him. Turn to Him now. Invite Him to take control of your marriage. As you pray, name your partner and each member of your family, asking the Lord to intervene and break through some long-standing barriers.

Summary

Complacency blinds us to reality, so wake up.

Knowledge sets us free, so listen up.

**Discernment prompts us to act courageously,
so step up.**

God loves us unconditionally, so look up.

I admit these four strong principles and no-nonsense applications may look simplistic on the page, but I assure you they aren't. Each point attempts to boil down a profound perspective into something memorable. After almost fifty-one years of marriage and forty-five years of family life, I can honestly tell you that these concepts are tried-and-true reminders that I still rely upon today. In fact, I would highly recommend rereading this chapter to cement them in your mind. Chances are good you'll see some things you missed the first time through.

As we examine the domestic scene in your home in much greater detail in the following chapters, we will stay close to the Scriptures. I will, of course, draw upon hard-earned lessons that have come by many hard knocks, and I will share whatever personal insights I have gained through the years. However, I need to say that I'm not the authority on marriage; God is. By the end of this book, I hope you will come away with a greater understanding of what God says about this mysterious bond, because His Word has been made clearer in your mind. I am confident in the power of the Bible to transform your marriage, your family, and even our entire society with its truth.

Erwin Lutzer illustrates the transforming power of God's Word on a culture this way:

> Eighteenth century Britain was in such a sad state of decline that Parliament had to be dismissed in the middle of the day because so many of its members were in a drunken stupor. Children were abandoned to die and immorality was rampant. The knowledge of God had all but faded from view. Mercifully, God reversed that trend through the preaching of John Wesley and George Whitefield. Some historians believe that it was that revival that spared Britain the bloody fate of France, torn by violent revolution.[3]

England had begun a moral slide, but God intervened. He used the courage of a few faithful men and women who said, "We will look to God, and He will give us direction and strength."

We can be like them. Let it begin with your marriage and mine.

Two

Getting Back on Target

———————— ∞ ————————

$\mathcal{I}$n 1947, Dr. Carle Zimmerman, a professor of sociology at Harvard University, published a book titled *Family and Civilization*. In this very technical work, he established an unmistakable correlation between the strength of the family and the strength of the culture. As the teeth of one gear mesh with another, the attitudes that undermine a family will ultimately bring down a nation.

Dr. Zimmerman identified three types of families, the last of which he called "atomistic." After a careful study of the world's great empires, he found that a nation of predominantly atomistic families rarely escapes extinction. I find his description of this type of family eerily prophetic:

> This type of family arises first as an extension of the ideas of freedom of the individual . . . Thus the individual is left more and more alone to do as he wishes.

At first the freedom becomes an incentive to economic gain. . . . But sooner or later the meaning of this freedom changes. The individual, having no guiding moral principles, changes the meaning of freedom from opportunity to license. Having no internal or external guides to discipline him, he becomes a gambler with life, always seeking greener pastures. When he comes to inevitable difficulty, he is alone in his misery. He wishes to pass his difficulties and his misery on to others. Consequently he continually helps to build up institutions to "remedy" his misery. He willingly follows any prophet (and they are mostly false ones) who comes along with a sure-cure nostrum for the diseases of the social system.[1]

Thus we witness the peculiar anomaly in that atomistic people, who seem to have given all for "this freedom," are the ones who create the most violent and bloodthirsty dictatorships.[2]

Here are six of the particular attitudes that Zimmerman states are typical of a society nearing its last days. Most of them have to do with marriage.

- Increased and rapid, easy, "causeless" divorce. [Guilty-and-innocent party theory became a pure fiction.]

- Elimination of the real meaning of the marriage ceremony.
- Rise of theories that companionate marriage or looser family forms would solve social ills. [A companionate marriage is one in which the couple agrees to just be companions, not to have children, not to commingle their finances, and divorce by mutual consent.]
- The refusal of many other people married under the older family form to maintain their traditions while other people escape these obligations. [The Greek and Roman mothers refused to stay home and bear children.]
- Breaking down of most inhibitions against adultery.
- Common acceptance of all forms of sex perversions.[3]

When I first began preparing to write this book, I promised the Lord that I would not become a prophet of doom and gloom but that I would instead strive to be an encouragement. That's my promise to you. But we need to start with a realistic perspective. In my previous chapter, I issued a call for us to "wake up." Each of these six trends Zimmerman explained has not only continued but accelerated. I'm sad to observe that people in our churches fare no better than the world at large. Statistics for divorce and infidelity are virtually the same for those who describe themselves as committed Christians as those who do not. I will admit that all of this runs a chill up my back as I look around me.

Fortunately, we have hope for two important reasons. First, God works through the minority—a remnant. A remnant is a group of godly people in the midst of an ungodly society. The majority of people may reject God's view of marriage, but God may choose to reverse those trends by the example of a faithful few. He's done that before . . . many times.

Second, poor decisions in the past do not prevent future good decisions. Remember this: *it's never too late to start doing what is right.* You may have made a mess of this marriage, another marriage, or even several marriages. Don't allow that to keep you from making your current situation—whether married or single—a tribute to God's grace. It's never too late to start anew! The same is true in any society; we can rise above the failures of the past by choosing God's way over our own.

I want you to see hope in these pages, even though our culture has strayed far from the truth and we've allowed ourselves to be dragged along after it. Biblical hope won't come by ignoring problems but by believing that God is bigger than any of them. No threat is too big for Him. Nothing takes Him by surprise. No sin is too much for

His power and grace. Our responsibility is to take a realistic look at our own attitudes and choices, compare them to His Word, and repent where necessary.

Interestingly, the principle word for sin in the New Testament is *hamartia,* which literally means "a missing of the mark." If we are to experience all the joy God intended for us personally, and if we hope to be the remnant that leads our culture toward the truth, we must get our families back on target—stop missing the mark. Obviously, that must begin with *your* marriage.

With that in mind, I want to turn your attention from history and sociology to God's Word—from the bleak to the sublime. It's when we come to God's Word that we gain fresh perspective.

MARRIAGE IS GOD'S INVENTION

Chapter 2 of Genesis is a story. If we are careful to examine the symbols and how the inspired author writes the story, we'll discover that marriage is God's invention. He intended this lifelong, exclusive union between a man and a woman to become the foundation upon which a family is built. This first of all human relationships goes all the way back to creation.

To set the context of the story, take note of the progression in Genesis 1:

God created light and declared it "good." (v. 4)

God created dry land and the seas and "saw that it was good." (v. 10)

He gave life to vegetation and "saw that it was good." (v. 12).

He hung the heavenly bodies in space and "saw that it was good." (v. 18)

He made sea creatures and birds and "saw that it was good." (v. 21)

He made land animals and "saw that it was good." (v. 25)

He saw all that He had made and declared it all "very good" (v. 31).

But then something surprising occurs in Genesis 2.

While the creation account in Genesis 1 includes the crafting of humans, it only does so in summary fashion. Genesis 2 rewinds the tape to allow us to see the creation of humanity in slow motion and in greater detail. After creating everything in the world and declaring it good, the Lord fashioned a single human, and for the first time in the Scriptures, He says, "It is *not* good" (Genesis 2:18;

emphasis added). Did He create the man incorrectly? No. "It is not good for the man *to be alone.*" The literal Hebrew is, "The man's being alone is not good."

God placed the solitary human male in a garden that would supply his every physical need, yet His evaluation was, in effect, "He still has a need." So the Creator said, "I will make him a helper suitable for him." Notice two words in particular: "helper" and "suitable."

Adam needed a helper. Now I can almost hear the gasps, but before we read too much English into the word *helper*, we need a little help from Hebrew grammar. "Helper" sounds menial, even a little pathetic. We think of one person having the knowledge and skill to accomplish a task while the "helper" merely makes the job easier. But that's not how the Hebrews used it. The word *ezer* has the idea of supplying something crucial that is lacking, and it most often refers to God. For example, Psalm 30:10 says, "Hear, O LORD, and be gracious to me; O LORD, be my *helper*." Psalm 54:4 declares, "Behold, God is my *helper*; the LORD is the sustainer of my soul."

"Helper" in the Hebrew mind is anything but menial. God saw Adam and determined that something crucial was missing. Humankind was incomplete. His aloneness was *not* good. We know from Genesis 1 that humans were to multiply, fill the earth, and rule over it. Adam was made for a purpose that he could not fulfill alone. The song of life was to be sung as a duet, in harmony, but Adam was only one voice. His solo wouldn't cut it.

Furthermore, only the right kind of voice would suffice. Notice that the helper must be a "suitable" helper or, more literally, "one according to his opposite" or "one corresponding to him." This second human creation would have to be a very different being than any that had been created. Observe what God did next:

> Out of the ground the LORD God formed every beast of the field and every bird of the sky, and brought them to the man to see what he would call them; and whatever the man called a living creature, that was its name. The man gave names to all the cattle, and to the birds of the sky, and to every beast of the field, but for Adam there was not found a helper *suitable* for him. (Genesis 2:19–20; emphasis added)

Now I admit that this looks very odd in the context of finding Adam a mate, but remember that God knew all along what He was going to do. This exercise was for Adam's benefit . . . and for ours as we read it. As the Lord paraded each kind of animal before Adam, the man would certainly have to recognize that each had a corresponding mate. But he also had to see that nothing in all of animal creation was a suitable companion for him. Something miraculous would have to take place. A completely different creature would have to be fashioned. And, whereas all other created beings were formed from the ground, take note of the very significant difference in the next verses:

> So the LORD God caused a deep sleep to fall upon the man, and he slept; then He took one of his ribs and closed up the flesh at that place. The LORD God fashioned into a woman the rib which He had taken from the man, and brought her to the man. The man said, "This is now bone of my bones, and flesh of my flesh; she shall be called Woman, because she was taken out of Man." (Genesis 2:21–23)

Matthew Henry's venerable commentary offers this observation that I find very poignant. He says, "The woman was *made of a rib out of the side of Adam;* not made out of his head to rule over him, nor out of his feet to be trampled upon by him, but out of his side to be equal with him, under his arm to be protected, and near his heart to be beloved."[4] He also notes, "If man is the head, she is the

33

crown, a crown to her husband, the crown of the visible creation. The man was dust refined, but the woman was dust double-refined, one remove further from the earth."[5]

Once Adam "recovered from surgery" he opened his eyes and saw the woman. The Hebrew is emphatic so that his first words should be translated, "Now, finally, *at last!*" She perfectly complemented his every strength and weakness the way no other creature could. Adam's declaration, "This is now bone of my bones, and flesh of my flesh," is the basis for a Hebrew expression describing closeness, oneness, or intimacy. It communicates that she is the fulfillment of everything he desired. And having seen every other creature God had made, he was in a good position to know! This is a magnificent scene played out in an idyllic setting, and it's the beginning of a wonderful love story.

Don't rush ahead into Genesis 3, or the serpent, or sin, or the Fall. Don't go there . . . not yet. Let your mind dwell for a time on the wonderful gift that God had given the first people: marriage, the harmonious blending of two lives in a pristine relationship that brought joy and fulfillment to both. Only God could create something so magnificent.

This is our target. Pure, uninhibited, unselfish, blissful union enjoyed by two people made for each other. No barriers. No issues. No awkwardness. No hang-ups. Just intimacy. Pause for a moment and use your mind's eye. Imagine the problems that they *didn't* have. Next, imagine how they would have behaved toward each other.

FOUR ESSENTIAL ELEMENTS FOR MARRIAGE

At the very end of this narrative, Moses writes a very significant statement that lays the foundation for marriage as God originally designed it to be. These words are so important that Jesus used them in His teaching on marriage (Matthew 19:5), as did Paul (Ephesians 5:31).

> For this reason a man shall leave his father and his mother, and be joined to his wife; and they shall become one flesh. And the man and his wife were both naked and were not ashamed. (Genesis 2:24–25)

In these two verses, we find four essential elements that hold a marriage together. Whenever I've worked with a couple having difficulties, almost without exception, I've found at least one or more of these elements missing or distorted. On the other hand, when I observe a good, healthy union, the couple usually has all four in place. For the sake of simplicity, I have boiled each element down to one word.

Severance

> For this reason a man shall *leave* his father and his
> mother . . . (Genesis 2:24; emphasis added)

The Hebrew word for "leave" is most often translated
"abandon." Now don't read into this more than God is
saying. He's not calling for the man and woman to disrespect their parents. Parents are not to be ignored or forgotten or given a cold shoulder. "Abandoning" here has
two important ideas in mind. The first has to do with primary allegiance. While continuing to honor and love parents, a wife comes first . . . a husband comes first.

My friend and colleague Dr. Frank Minirth puts it
well:

> "Leaving and cleaving" may feel like a betrayal and
> carry with it a fair amount of guilt. "How can I turn
> my back on the people that birthed me, fed me, loved
> me, and protected me for so many years?" For-
> tunately, the truth of the Bible gives you permission
> to devote yourself entirely to your new family unit,
> guilt free. Failure to do this will eventually strain
> every relationship you have. Besides, giving preemi-
> nence to your new family doesn't require you to love

your old family any less. Quite the opposite—you can love them twice as much![6]

"Abandoning" first means the man and woman switch their primary allegiance. Second, "abandoning" the family of origin has to do with dependence. The man and woman no longer look to Mom and Dad for support or to have their needs met. Instead they begin to look to each other. That doesn't mean that the couple can't or shouldn't accept help. In fact, it has been a particular joy for Cynthia and me to help each of our children purchase homes as a major part of our inheritance to them. We offered, but they didn't expect it. We assisted and gave them gifts, but they and their mates depend upon themselves. The only way to have a truly autonomous, self-sustaining household is for the man and woman to sever themselves from their original families.

I'm amazed to see people—and I don't mean young ones—who still haven't left Mom and Dad. Though married to a mate, they still cling to the original family, emotionally tied to one or both of their parents. This reminds me of a little folk song we used to sing as kids. It's called "Billy Boy." I can't resist doing a little exposition of the song.

Oh, where have you been,
Billy Boy, Billy Boy?
Oh, where have you been,
Charming Billy?
I have been to seek a wife,
She's the joy of my life,
She's a young thing
And cannot leave her mother.

Each stanza ends with, "She's a young thing and cannot leave her mother." So I wondered how old she is. As I read through the song, I found my answer!

How old is she,
Billy Boy, Billy Boy?
How old is she,
Charming Billy?
Three times six and four times seven,
Twenty-eight and eleven,
She's a young thing
And cannot leave her mother.

Three times six (18), plus four times seven (28), plus 28 and 11, for a grand total of 85 years! Billy Boy's girl-friend is an octogenarian! *Give it up, Billy!* She's not the one for you. If she can't leave her mother by now, trust me, she never will! Furthermore, she won't be much of a marriage partner.

Now, to be fair, I've seen just as many men who won't cut the apron strings as women whose hearts belong to Daddy. I've seen women with such a bond with Mom there's no room for anyone else and men who depend upon Dad's checkbook as much as their own. Unless both partners in a marriage deliberately "leave" their old families behind, their marriage can't possibly succeed.

Permanence

. . . and be joined to his wife. (Genesis 2:24)

The second element is permanence. Permanence naturally follows severance. Observe, by the way, that each element builds upon the one before it. One must leave the original family before he or she can be truly joined with a mate. When I see the Hebrew word for "joined," I think of glue. As of this writing, workmen are completing the woodwork in a new home for Cynthia and me (and it will be our last!). They use a special glue that will join two pieces of wood together so permanently that, when stressed, the wood will splinter and snap before breaking the bond.

This is the same word used by Ruth when pledging her

devotion to Naomi after both women had been widowed. When used figuratively of people, it describes absolute devotion, absolute loyalty, uncompromising affection and love. This is not clinging-vine dependence. This is devotion—two healthy, emotionally strong people choosing to stick together no matter what happens. Jesus took the words of Genesis a step further. (He's God. He can do that!) He said, "What therefore God has joined together, let no man separate" (Mark 10:9).

What if you're beyond your first marriage? You might be thinking, *Chuck, you're talking to someone else. I've already gone through one marriage (maybe several), and it didn't work out. These words are too late for me!* To you, I say, "Stop. Wait. We're talking about *now* and where you go from *here*. Not the past. The past is a different subject. Apply this to the marriage you have *now*. Determine that this marriage is permanent. God has joined you; let no one and let nothing separate you."

Cynthia and I both came from homes where our parents stuck it out. Neither had perfect marriages; in fact, both experienced difficulties. All marriages do! But both sets of parents remained committed to their vows, and we were better able to remain committed to ours because of them.

Your commitment to the permanence of your marriage

will be a legacy you leave your children that will reap benefits that you cannot possibly foresee.

Unity

. . . and they shall become one flesh. (Genesis 2:24)

The third element is unity. Not uniformity, but unity. Eve was not created to become a female Adam. She wasn't a clone. Nor was she supposed to have any less identity than Adam. In fact, Moses chose between two Hebrew words for "one." The term he chose is *echad*, which, according to a very respected lexicon, "stresses unity while recognizing diversity within that oneness."[7] A good example of that is Exodus 26:6.

> You shall make fifty clasps of gold, and join the curtains to one another with the clasps so that the tabernacle will be a unit.

Literally, it says, "so that the tabernacle will be one." The word Moses used for "one flesh" is a complex unity. Not a melting of two personalities to form one, but two individuals living and working in concert with common values and shared goals. Unity is diversity brought into harmony.

I especially appreciate an illustration from the book *Love Is a Choice*. It pictures a figure-skating couple gliding across the ice. The man and woman intertwine their arms and legs, spinning and twirling in perfect synchronization with the music. Their movements are individual, different, yet carefully choreographed so that you think of them as one. Then suddenly they part ways and move in opposite directions, spin in perfect unison, then come together again.[8] This is a beautiful picture of two people living as "one flesh."

I often find that when the "one flesh" unity is misapplied, one partner controls the other. The controlling partner fails to give the other freedom to be. He or she allows no room for the other to cultivate gifts, develop talents, or enjoy the natural strengths that God provides. There's no room for disagreement without conflict. There's no tolerance for anything that doesn't benefit or involve the couple.

I almost ruined my own marriage as a result of my behavior during our first ten years together. I expected Cynthia to be a female Chuck. Can you think of anything more miserable than to have someone try to mold you into a copy of himself or herself? I wanted her to have my opinions. I wanted her to have my interests. I wanted her to think the same things, develop the same tastes, solve problems the way I did. Why? Because it was the right way to be!

I'll never forget one particular dark evening in New England. We were trying to make a ministry work, and I was at the end of my wits when Cynthia said, with tears in her eyes, "You know, honey, I'd like you to stop saying in public that we are partners. That may make you feel good and look good, but it's not true."

"Yes, it is," I said.

"No, it isn't," she responded.

"YES, it *is*."

"NO, IT'S NOT!"

With that, she walked out, climbed the stairs, and closed the door to our bedroom. I sat down at the kitchen table and did a painful review of the habits I had formed and the controlling, almost neurotic demands I had put on her. I thought of some areas where I put her in bondage to every jot and tittle I expected, and how my demeanor toward her had become critical and harsh.

After some time had passed and I realized how I had blown it, I went upstairs to find her crying. I sat on the side of the bed and said, "You're right . . . and it has to change."

That led to nearly four years of the hardest work we have ever done as a couple. I had to face my stubbornness and unwillingness to bend. I had to open my eyes to things I didn't want to admit about myself. But the reward was incredible. I still led the home, but with much more freedom, giving plenty of room for Cynthia to be herself. Little by little, she began to feel my love and growing respect. She felt that I believed in her and that I was in her corner. And in the process, I discovered a woman within Cynthia that I had never known before. The woman who emerged inspired respect in me that I didn't have before. I began to look for new ways to affirm her and honor her.

As more years passed, we started a little radio ministry called Insight for Living. Quickly, I realized that if this ministry was going to survive and flourish, Cynthia would have to lead it. I didn't have the time or the inclination or the skills necessary to pull it off. So she very graciously added that to her other duties as pastor's wife (one of the toughest jobs on earth) and mother of four children (even tougher!).

As the ministry grew, it was obvious that she was the right choice. I often attend meetings where she tells the story of IFL's history. I distinctly remember one time, years ago, when I heard her say, "By the way, the best part of all of this is that my husband is my partner." I thought, *What a great word: partner. This is so good.* Fifteen years earlier that wasn't true, but how far we had come. By then, I knew we were individuals working in harmony. We were "one flesh." We enjoyed unity . . . a true partnership.

Intimacy

> And the man and his wife were both naked and were
> not ashamed. (Genesis 2:25)

The man and woman leave their respective families (sever-ance), they commit themselves to each other (permanence), become one in terms of purpose and direction and mutual support (unity), and they enjoy an exclusive, privileged knowledge of each other (intimacy). Each element prepares the marriage for the next. Ultimately, intimacy is what every couple longs for. It's the grand prize—the reward—for all the effort we invest in our marriage.

The man and woman were naked and were not ashamed. Neither thought of covering anything because they had no self-consciousness, no shame, no fear of ridicule, no hang-ups, no embarrassment, no emotional hurts from former abuse or poor choices. Think of it! Nothing diseased or malformed or scarred or dysfunctional. Each was entirely focused on the delight and pleasure of the other. They enjoyed a free-flowing intimacy in many areas of their relationship that was uninhibited by self-interest. And the sexual union must have been more pleasant and fulfilling that anything we can imagine.

The late J. Grant Howard says it well in his book *The Trauma of Transparency.*

In Genesis 2:25 both partners are described as naked, yet without any sense of shame. This does not mean that they had no sexual desires. It simply means that they had not learned that sexual desire could be directed toward evil ends. They looked upon the sexual organs in the same way we regard the hands or the face. They were comfortable with each other. There were no barriers between them. They were ready, willing, able and needing to communicate with each other. . . . Here, for the moment, was that delicately balanced combination of truth and transparency that the world now struggles to understand and achieve.[9]

Unfortunately, many people confuse intimacy with sex. I always caution unmarried men and women to be careful with the powerful effects of touch. Sex is not intimacy. It's designed by God to be the product of intimacy. Sex too easily mimics genuine intimacy, and if you put it first, you'll soon discover that it's all you have between you. Intimacy involves sharing on multiple levels. Intimacy is shared discussion, shared silence, shared history, shared trials and heartbreaks, shared sorrow and grief, shared joy, and shared commitment. All of those things are shared completely and at great risk. This level of intimacy requires immense trust and enormous vulnerability.

When couples are able to enjoy complete intimacy, each partner can fulfill his or her primary responsibility in the marriage—and the responsibilities are different for the man and the woman. Based on hours of study in God's Word, here are what I believe to be the primary obligations of each partner:

The wife's primary responsibility is to know herself so well and to respect herself so much that she gives herself to her husband without hesitation.

The husband's primary responsibility is to love his Lord so deeply and to accept himself so completely that he gives himself to his wife without conditions.

I won't take time to develop these principles here as I have devoted an entire chapter to them in my book *The Grace Awakening*. I offer them here in order to ask you some important and direct questions. How far off-target are you? How difficult is it to fulfill your primary responsibility in the marriage? If you're normal, you'll have to admit that it's very difficult, at least part of the time. Why? Genesis 3. Sin ruins *everything*.

INTIMACY LOST

Before we have time to swoon over the romance of chapter 2, the tempter abruptly appears in Genesis 3. Read the following without a break:

> And the man and his wife were both naked and were not ashamed. Now the serpent . . . (Genesis 2:25–3:1)

He arrives on the scene with his soothing, reassuring voice, plays upon the curiosity of the wife and then her husband, and they eat of the forbidden tree. The sequence happens quickly. Moses tells this part of the story using four, rapid-fire verbs: she took, she ate, she gave, he ate. And once that first sin was committed, *everything* crashed. The changes almost make your head spin.

> Then the eyes of both of them were opened, and they knew that they were naked; and they sewed fig leaves together and made themselves loin coverings. (Genesis 3:7)

Now, Adam and Eve weren't blind before they ate, but afterward, they saw everything from a completely different perspective. Remember? *Everything* changed! Take note of the first thing they noticed: " and they *knew* they were *naked.*" In Genesis 2 their perspective was so turned outward from self that the thought of nakedness had never crossed their conscious minds. But after sinning, something profoundly sickening occurred within each. The innocence and intimacy of Genesis 2 are gone.

I note at least three changes in character that afflicted the first marriage. And these challenges threaten yours and mine today.

Self-Consciousness

First, *they became self-conscious and self-absorbed.* Rather than enjoying the uninhibited, naked vulnerability of their partner, they became shamefully aware of their own nakedness. Adam stopped caring for Eve's needs and focused on his. Eve did the same.

Isolation

Second, *they withdrew from each other.* Before sin twisted their character, they enjoyed harmony and unity and intimacy. But after their disobedience, their minds were darkened and their wills turned toward self-preservation. Their nakedness in this story is not merely physical; it's symbolic as well. The aprons they fashioned for themselves were made to cover their nakedness not from each other but from God. But the effect is the same. In their shame, they pull back their emotions and limit their trust.

Fear

> They heard the sound of the LORD God walking in the garden in the cool of the day, and the man and his wife hid themselves from the presence of the LORD God among the trees of the garden. (Genesis 3:8)

Third, *they ran from God*. After sinning, Adam and Eve felt different emotions and experienced the world with an altered perception. Before, they saw everything as God saw it: good. But just as sin caused them to withdraw from each other, sin put them at odds with their God.

Unfortunately, verse 8 uses Hebrew word pictures that are very difficult to translate into English. Most translations give you the impression that God came strolling into the garden with His hands in His pockets, whistling a tune, hoping to bump into Adam and Eve, completely unaware of their sin until He couldn't find them. Part of the problem comes from a likely mistranslation of the original text. The word translated "cool" comes from *ruah*, the Hebrew term usually translated "wind." But "wind of the day" doesn't sound right.

Recent research suggests that the root word commonly assumed to be "day" might actually be the term for "storm."[10] If this is correct, the verse would read: "They heard the sound of the LORD God moving into the garden on the wind of a storm, and the man and his wife hid themselves from the presence of the LORD God among the trees of the garden."

WHAT NOT TO DO IN THE FACE OF WRONGDOING

Not only did Adam and Eve lose the intimacy between them, but they also lost intimacy with their Creator. The Lord's coming to meet Adam and Eve was anything but casual. He came in His wrath to confront the first humans with their disobedience, so they ran in fear from Him.

While they were right to fear God, having put themselves at odds with Him, they were foolish to think they could hide from Him. He sees all and knows all. Yet notice that the Lord asks questions of Adam and Eve:

Then the LORD God called to the man, and said to him, "Where are you?" He said, "I heard the sound of You in the garden, and I was afraid because I was naked; so I hid myself." And He said, "Who told you that you were naked? Have you eaten from the tree of which I commanded you not to eat?" The man said, "The woman whom You gave to be with me, she gave me from the tree, and I ate." Then the LORD God said to the woman, "What is this you have done?" And the woman said, "The serpent deceived me, and I ate." (Genesis 3:9–13)

God is all-knowing. He didn't ask these questions because He didn't know what had happened. His conversation with the original couple was an act of grace. He didn't have to confront them. He could have passed judgment without a word, but He chose to confront their sin openly. With each question, the Lord gave Adam, then Eve, an opportunity to come clean with the whole truth, repent, and ask forgiveness. But with each question, the man and woman failed to respond as they should. In just a matter of minutes, they are completely different. Sin took an immediate toll.

We can take an important lesson from Adam and Eve at this point. We can never regain the innocence and the intimacy of Genesis 2. Yet, all is not lost. We can enjoy intimacy, but only as we respond to wrongdoing constructively.

In the encounter between God and the first couple, I

see two responses to sin that destroy intimacy. These are important to study as we discover how we can enjoy intimacy after the Fall of Genesis 3.

Deception

The first destructive response to wrongdoing is deception—a spiritual, moral fig leaf. Let's face it, when given the opportunity to avoid blame, we'd rather lie than admit the truth. We'll even cut the truth into pieces and take only what we have to in order to minimize exposure.

"Adam, why did you hide from Me?"

"I was afraid because I was naked." (A half-truth, and the first opportunity bypassed.)

"Who told you that you were naked?"

I always smile a little at this question. I would think that the cool breeze blowing across his skin might be a clue, but, as usual, there's something more behind God's question. The question is really, "When did this become an issue? You've been naked for how long now? What changed?" Then He nudged Adam a little closer to the truth. "Have you eaten from the tree of which I commanded you not to eat?" This leads to another response to sin that destroys intimacy.

Blame Shifting

The second intimacy killer is blame shifting.

The man said, "The woman whom You gave to be with me, she gave me from the tree, and I ate." (Genesis 3:12)

This must have crushed Eve's heart. The man who called her "bone of my bones, and flesh of my flesh" betrayed her to save himself. I can imagine she never looked at him the same again. Then to save her own skin, Eve also diverted responsibility.

Then the LORD God said to the woman, "What is this you have done?" And the woman said, "The serpent deceived me, and I ate." (Genesis 3:13)

RECOVERING INTIMACY

Clearly, we live in a world twisted by sin. Everything was affected by Adam and Eve's choice to disobey God, marriage included. If we are to recover the institution of marriage for our society and intimacy for ourselves, we must deal with reality constructively. Confess the truth of any situation and accept responsibility. No matter what happens, however bad we may look, or how awful the consequences, refuse to lie or shift the blame.

Once the sin was committed, imagine the difference in

Adam and Eve's relationship if the conversation had gone
this way instead:

Then the LORD God called to the man, and said to
him, "Where are you?"

And Adam said, "I'm here, Lord. I've been waiting
for you. I have something to confess."

"Please do."

Adam began to weep. "The thing is, Lord, I have
sinned. I clearly remember your telling me that I must
not eat of the tree of the knowledge of good and evil,
but I did anyway. I have no excuse. Please forgive me."

God then asked, "The woman I gave to be your
helper . . . did she eat as well?"

Adam stepped forward. "She did. We both have
disobeyed you. Please have mercy on us . . . for her
sake especially."

So much for dreaming. What really happened was
tragedy on parade.

PROBING FOR THE TRUTH

How's the intimacy in your marriage? Do you want to get
your family back on target and keep it on target? Take

your eyes off your mate. Quit hoping a counselor will "straighten out" your spouse. Stop blaming your kids . . . or your job . . . or your circumstances. Look at yourself. Accept complete responsibility for where you've blown it. Own it, confess it, repent of it, and determine to do the hard work of correcting it.

Start now.

Recognizing the Lord's original plan for marriage and acknowledging how we've missed the mark are crucial first steps to recovering intimacy with our mates. As we take responsibility for how we've blown it in the past and begin taking steps to get back on target, we give them hope. Furthermore, this is the same hope we offer our society as a faithful remnant.

It's never too late to start doing what's right.

Three

Symphony of Survival in the Key of "C"

$\sigma^{\!\!\top}$

I am more than seventy years old, I have been married for more than fifty years, and I have been in ministry for more than forty years; so when I speak to a twenty-first-century audience I find it difficult to sound like something other than a nineteenth-century preacher. I discovered that there's a word for guys like me, a preacher who still believes the Bible, who thinks we need to adjust our lives to the principles of Scripture rather than twist the text to justify our choices. Someone told me that when I'm not around, a few people call me a "dinosaur." So, as often happens, my curiosity sent me to the dictionary:

> di•no•saur \di•ne•sor\ *noun* 3 : one that is impractically large, out-of-date, or obsolete[1]

I was admittedly a little dismayed, but I found it easier to stomach than the Greek etymology of the word: *deinos* +

sauros . . . "terrifying lizard." After I mentioned this to a group of people, a man offered me a little comfort. "I wouldn't feel too bad if I were you. One of my grandkids calls me a Neanderthal!" I'm afraid to look that one up.

Aside from being "impractically large," I'm proud to be a dinosaur, especially if that means remaining faithful to God's Word—believing it, studying it, diligently preparing and passionately delivering messages that reflect its timeless principles. As a postmodern generation gropes for truth while denying that it exists, it's reassuring to cling to what I know to be reliable.

Unfortunately, some tend to mistake this confidence for arrogance. Such are our times. G. K. Chesterton saw the early signs of this many years ago when he wrote:

> But what we suffer from today is humility in the wrong place. Modesty has moved from the organ of ambition. Modesty has settled upon the organ of conviction; where it was never meant to be. A man was meant to be doubtful about himself, but undoubting about the truth; this has been exactly reversed. . . . We are on the road to reproducing a race of men too mentally modest to believe in the multiplication table.[2]

We need to be absolutely sure of what we believe, especially if our marriages are going to stand the test of time. I don't claim to be the author or the sole possessor of truth. But I can say with assurance that I embrace the truth without apology or hesitation. Many centuries old and available in almost any bookstore, it's full of unusual names and stories too bizarre to be fiction, preserving ideas as profound as they are ancient. In the pages of the Bible, we find principles for living—unique in their presentation, plainly wrapped in elegant simplicity, yet deeply mysterious and profound.

These principles are reliable. We can trust them to preserve us and our relationships however unsophisticated they may appear to the intellectual mind. The text of the Bible was originally written in Hebrew and Aramaic and Greek, authored and assembled over hundreds of years by a variety of people—all of them human and therefore sinful—yet God has miraculously preserved the accuracy and relevance of its truth. Consequently, it has the authority to instruct any society, in any era, in any region.

God's Word will help people of any age, any social status, in any life stage or circumstance: married, single, widowed, divorced, multiple divorced, abused, broken, terrorized, hurting, struggling, fighting for survival, prosperous, happy, healthy, joyful, guilty, grieving, or dying. In more than fifty years of study, I have never found an irrelevant principle in the pages of Scripture. Anytime I have found one to fail me, it was because I failed to understand, appreciate, and apply it. In the end, I discovered that I had failed the principle rather than the other way around. And the consequences were usually grave.

In the previous chapter, we discussed four essential elements found in Genesis 2:24–25 that define biblical marriage: severance, permanence, unity, and intimacy. Not one of them is automatic. They all require deliberate attention and personal effort. This chapter will focus on permanence and the principle that will ensure it. It's simple, straightforward, highly effective, and, like me, something of a dinosaur. The principle can be summed up in a single word: *commitment.*

COMMITMENT:
THE KEY TO A PERMANENT MARRIAGE

There's nothing fancy in the word commitment—a simple word describing a simple concept. Now as a realist, I recognize that simple doesn't mean easy. Nor am I so naive and rigid in my theology as to ignore the fact that we live in a world twisted by evil as a result of Genesis 3, and certain circumstances call for separation and even allow for divorce. But that's not where we begin. One author noted that divorce, like embalming, is not something you want to apply prematurely. I discuss the biblical grounds for divorce (which God hates nonetheless) in *Getting Through the Tough*

Stuff, so we'll not dwell on it here. I want to focus on the reasons to *stay* rather than the reasons to *escape*.

Commitment is a biblical mandate for marriage. And like all biblical mandates, it requires faith to see beyond the immediate and offers unseen rewards when obeyed. Take it from a guy who's been married for more than fifty years: that one-flesh union won't maintain itself, but it's worth the effort. You *learn* to become a unit. You stay with it through all of the sinful struggles and annoying habits, plodding through those hard times when you would like nothing more than to call it quits and disappear. Then, after you've made it though a number of crises together, you realize in unguarded moments that you're glad you stuck it out. You're glad you made it work. And you're especially glad your partner didn't walk out.

As we examine commitment, the key to permanence, three couples in the Bible come to mind. Each faced a particular challenge and has something to teach us by their example.

THE CHALLENGE OF CONSEQUENCES (ADAM AND EVE)

The marriage of Adam and Eve in Genesis 2, like most weddings, took place under ideal circumstances. But unlike any other marriage, they were married by God in a pristine environment, in a world without sin. "The man and his wife were both naked and were not ashamed" (Genesis 2:25). Nothing inhibited their intimacy. No hint of selfishness tainted their caring for each other. No outburst of anger led them into a verbal fight. Then sin changed all of that. After their disobedience, God detailed the consequences of their tragic choice:

> To the woman he said, "I will greatly increase your labor pains; with pain you will give birth to children. You will want to control your husband, but he will dominate you." But to Adam he said, "Because you obeyed your wife and ate from the tree about which I commanded you, 'You must not eat from it,' cursed is the ground thanks to you; in painful toil you will eat of it all the days of your life. It will produce thorns and thistles for you, but you will eat the grain of the field. By the sweat of your brow you will eat food until you return to the ground, for out of it you were taken; for you are dust, and to dust you will return."
>
> So the LORD God expelled him from the orchard in Eden to cultivate the ground from which he had been taken. (Genesis 3:16–19, 23 NET)

This is what theologians call "the Fall." It affected the nature of humankind, their relationships, and even the world around them. Nothing is destroyed, but everything is damaged. Because of sin, there's something wrong with everything. But notice what did *not* change. The man and woman still bore the image of God, though that image became a contorted one. They were still to care for the earth, but it would resist their efforts. Humanity's relationship with the ground would be hampered by difficulty—thistles and weeds—and the soil would only yield produce through sweat and toil. The same would be true of their relationship. They remained husband and wife and were still to multiply and fill the earth. Yet what had been an easy, natural intimacy became complicated by fear and defensiveness, selfishness and withdrawal. And the awful effects of sin would continue to haunt them.

They were driven from the Garden of Eden, never again to see the idyllic place of their pairing and first wonderful days of their marriage. They would bury a son, the victim of murder at the hands of his older brother. They would see their eldest son banished from all social contact, cursed to live as a vagrant because of his crime. And, if my calculations are correct, Adam lived long enough to attend the birth of Noah, which means that the first couple saw the steady moral decline of the world's inhabitants (their own descendants) to the point that God regretted creating people at all.

If anyone could cite difficulties as a reason to end their marriage, Adam and Eve could. Yet through it all, they remained together. We learn from the marriage of Adam and Eve that the harsh consequences of evil—the sin-corrupted image of God in humans and the sin-twisted world—do not make marriage impossible. Difficult, but not impossible.

You may have come from a home so unbelievably horrific that few can comprehend the damage it has done to you. You may bear deep scars of abuse and mistreatment— emotional, physical, perhaps even sexual. You may have come from a household where you never knew the safety and security of parents who loved each other and loved you. Maybe you haven't seen a healthy marriage modeled for you, which means you don't even know how to begin building one. Maybe your romantic life is one characterized by a long string of broken relationships with poorly chosen partners and sabotage at the first sign of genuine intimacy.

If you are married and this describes you—even just a little—take heart. Healing is available. It won't be easy, but you'll never find it by running. If you are married and if your safety isn't threatened, choose to remain committed to your mate as an important first step.

The Challenge of Conflict
(Hosea and Gomer)

I can think of no greater challenge to marriage than infidelity. So serious is the damage that the Lord considers it a breach of the marital bond and permits divorce (see Matthew 19:8–9). However, that's not to say that divorce is required or even inevitable. Consider the marriage of the prophet Hosea.

Many centuries after Adam and Eve, long after Moses, the judges, and King David, Israel had been living in Canaan. But sin and idolatry had plunged the nation into civil war, dividing north from south, with the Northern Kingdom worshiping other gods. To convict the Hebrew people of their spiritual infidelity, God chose to use the life of His prophet Hosea—not only his words and his writing, but his *marriage*.

> When the LORD first spoke through Hosea, the LORD said to Hosea, "Go, take to yourself a wife of harlotry and have children of harlotry; for the land commits flagrant harlotry, forsaking the LORD." (Hosea 1:2)

What an amazing command! This is a costly object lesson for Hosea and introduces one of the most difficult books of Scripture to interpret and to read. To get His point across, the Lord put Himself in the role of a jilted spouse and walked with His servant Hosea through the horrifying experience of marital infidelity. The Lord knows the sting of betrayal firsthand and on a scale we can barely comprehend.

> So he went and took Gomer the daughter of Diblaim, and she conceived and bore him a son. (Hosea 1:3)

Scholars cannot say for sure whether Gomer was a harlot before marriage or became one some years later. The phrase "wife of harlotry" seems to describe what she would become since she was not a wife at the time Hosea chose her and the "children of harlotry" had not yet been born. So we might say he picked a nice, Jewish girl to marry.

> Then she conceived again and gave birth to a daughter. And the LORD said to him, "Name her Loruhamah, for I will no longer have compassion on the house of Israel, that I would ever forgive them." (Hosea 1:6)

The name of the daughter means literally "no compassion." The names of the children are symbolic, which was very common for the time. The name of each child describes God's attitude toward Israel. The boy's name, Jezreel, points to the nation's violent behavior. The girl's name warns that the Lord's patience with wayward Israel is running out. Then Gomer bears another boy.

> When she had weaned Lo-ruhamah, she conceived and gave birth to a son. And the LORD said, "Name him Lo-ammi, for you are not My people and I am not your God." (Hosea 1:8–9)

Lo-ammi means "not My people." At this point, Gomer apparently left Hosea to live a life of prostitution. In a very real sense, she was no longer his wife. Chapter 2 describes Israel in these same terms, which reflected Gomer's behavior. She gave herself to multiple men, living off the money she bartered for sex. Meanwhile, Hosea was left a single parent with the responsibilities of rearing the children alone. He was a prophet of God who had to carry on with ministry despite his embarrassment before others and the deep hurt he felt. I have a preacher friend who calls this story "A Scandal in the Parsonage." Indeed it was.

At this point, it's safe to say that the marriage was over. Put bluntly, Gomer became a whore on the street, giving Hosea every moral cause to divorce her. The Bible doesn't tell us whether or not he did this. Nevertheless, her actions made it clear that she was no longer living with him as his wife.

Then something remarkable happens in chapter 3. We have no way of knowing how long Gomer was gone. She may have lived as a prostitute for many years, having one long, sensual party until no one wanted her for sex anymore. Aging, used up, and pathetic, she could have sold herself into slavery to survive—a common practice for the destitute. It was then that the Lord instructed Hosea to do the unthinkable.

> The Lord said to me, "Go, show love to your wife again, even though she loves another man and continually commits adultery. Likewise, the Lord loves the Israelites although they turn to other gods and love to offer raisin cakes to idols." So I paid fifteen shekels of silver and about seven bushels of barley to purchase her. (Hosea 3:1–2 NET)

This was the normal price for a slave.

> Then I told her, "You must live with me many days; you must not commit adultery or have sexual intercourse with another man, and I also will wait for you." (Hosea 3:3 NET)

I find his words to her utterly remarkable.

I don't want to lose sight of the bigger issue here. This is, first, a picture of the Lord's relationship with Israel. Hosea 9:9 says, "[The nation has] gone deep in depravity." On a national scale, they left the Lord to prostitute themselves with false gods. And, like Hosea, the Lord, in grace, purchased them back at great cost to Himself and restored them to their former place of honor as His people. (This is clearly a foreshadowing of what Christ would do for you and me.)

What Hosea did for his unfaithful and undeserving wife is a prime example of uncommon grace. He was directed to do this by God because he had a very unique duty as the Lord's spokesman before Israel. So his case is special. However, it does represent God's highest, greatest desire in such cases. This is important for all of us to keep in mind— for those who have suffered the betrayal of marital infidelity *and* for those who haven't.

I want to write these next few lines very sensitively. Please read them slowly and carefully. If you are the victim of marital infidelity—probably the greatest challenge to a marriage—you are not *required* to remain married. God does permit divorce in this case. However, if your mate is genuinely repentant and willing to do the difficult work of rebuilding the trust, let me encourage you to consider

69

applying uncommon grace. Hosea did . . . and so can you. While you are entitled to walk away, you may be forfeiting greater happiness and healing that comes by extending grace than by turning away and claiming your right. It's a more difficult path, admittedly. It's riskier. It requires immense faith and enormous forgiveness. But unseen rewards could be greater than you can imagine. Divorce will not erase the pain and the damage the infidelity has done to your spirit. You must heal either way. The question is, how and with whom will you heal?

For those who haven't suffered this horrible tragedy, Hosea's example demonstrates that no marriage is "too dead" for the Lord to restore. All marriages have at least one thing in common: *they all involve sinful people.* Sooner or later, one spouse will sin against the other . . . and sin big. Sin, forgiveness, healing, and rebuilding trust challenges the commitment of every marriage. If the Lord can put the marriage of Hosea and Gomer back together, He can keep yours from falling apart in the face of just about anything.

THE CHALLENGE OF CIRCUMSTANCES
(JOSEPH AND MARY)

A third example can be found tucked away in the first chapter of Matthew's Gospel. It's a familiar story told every Christmas, but I want to look at this story through a different lens.

> Now the birth of Jesus Christ was as follows: when His mother Mary had been betrothed to Joseph, before they came together she was found to be with child by the Holy Spirit. (Matthew 1:18)

According to the Jewish custom of the time, Mary and Joseph were formally united by a marriage contract but were required to wait one year before consummating the marriage, celebrating the official public wedding, and setting up their own household. The contract was so binding, however, that only a legal divorce could break it. Mary was considered Joseph's wife in every respect. During this period, before Joseph ever touched her sexually, Mary became pregnant.

We know from Luke's account that Mary was made aware of the plan; an angel explained to her what was going to happen. The Holy Spirit miraculously conceived her child. However, Joseph knew nothing ahead of time. All he knew was that Mary was pregnant with a child that was not his. Take note of his response:

> And Joseph her husband, being a righteous man and not wanting to disgrace her, planned to send her away

secretly. But when he had considered this, behold, an angel of the Lord appeared to him in a dream, saying, "Joseph, son of David, do not be afraid to take Mary as your wife; for the Child who has been conceived in her is of the Holy Spirit. She will bear a Son; and you shall call His name Jesus, for He will save His people from their sins." (Matthew 1:19–21)

Try hard to identify with what Joseph must have felt. He discovered that his wife is pregnant, drew the only conclusion that made sense—adultery, and decided to opt for a quiet divorce. Mary probably tried to explain, but let's face it, her story is unbelievable. "Yes, I'm pregnant; no, I didn't have sex with another man. God caused all of this, Joseph."

Come on! No man would have believed that.

Fortunately, Joseph soon received confirmation from God that she had told him the truth. Then came the decision. He had to know that any hope for a normal marriage would be frustrated by the inevitable wagging of tongues. The neighborhood gossip network in the small town of Nazareth would be working overtime. Everyone in his community could count to nine, and when Mary shows up at the synagogue in maternity clothes a little sooner than expected, everyone would reach the same conclusion. Talk about a scandal! We know this happened because, later on in Jesus's ministry, his enemies in the temple would say with biting sarcasm, "*We* were not born of fornication" (John 8:41; emphasis added).

Joseph and Mary would have to rest confidently in the truth of their innocence and find contentment in that. No one would believe the truth no matter how hard they tried to convince them. Whispers and snickering and jokes and scorn would be their closest and most enduring companions. This would either draw them together, or it would become a wedge. They would either seek opposite corners of the house or turn toward each other for strength. Stop and think. Everything hinged on their commitment to each other.

If the couple remains committed, their marriage will endure the strangest circumstances. No one outside the couple may understand (including their parents), and the married pair may be left with no external support, but if they remain committed to each other and the covenant they made with God, the marriage will survive. In fact, the intimacy may even grow sweeter as the two share a perspective that no one else on earth would appreciate.

You may be faced with an unusual set of circumstances

that challenges your marriage from the outside. Having been in ministry for more than four decades, I've helped a lot of folks going through terrible times. So I know how difficult life can be when dealing with problems in a marriage. Nevertheless, in all these years I've never seen one marriage get worse when the partners redouble their commitment to each other. The problems may not go away, but the marriage only gets stronger.

An Important Disclaimer

I feel the need to insert a qualification to everything I have written so far. I want to remain biblical to the core but without being so rigid as to ignore some ugly realities. In fact, the Bible doesn't ignore them either. My heart has been broken more than a few times when I witnessed situations in which a divorce averted certain disaster.

If you or your children are in danger of physical harm, you have a moral obligation to put an end to the relationship as it exists now. Reconciliation or remarriage are issues that can be dealt with in due time. For the sake of yourself and your children, get out, get away, and get help. Divorce may or may not be the right course of action, depending upon your mate's willingness or ability to change. But unless and until the marriage is safe, depart and *remain* apart. The Lord never intended your commitment to be your destruction. God is firm, but He isn't cruel.

If your married partner is using illegal drugs, I highly recommend that you at least separate until he or she has demonstrated the ability to remain clean and sober for a number of months. Remain committed. This is unfortunately a part of the vows, but you would be foolish to live in the same household.

If your mate is committing adultery, continues the sinful behavior, and remains unrepentant, your commitment to the marriage may actually discourage reconciliation. This sounds strange, but I encourage you to read a fine book by my good friend Dr. James Dobson titled *Love Must Be Tough*. He goes into careful detail I'll not attempt to do here. I must warn you . . . it won't be easy. Doing what's right in difficult situations is never easy.

KEEPING THE MARRIAGE UNDER LOCK AND KEY

If marriage is going to survive, commitment is priority one. Very little else you do in a marriage will matter if you haven't determined to stay in it. Whether the challenge is consequences, conflict, or circumstances, the key to maintaining a lifelong marriage is commitment. It's a choice that doesn't change with feelings, doesn't depend on good fortune or even the attitude of your mate. Commitment says to your partner, "I know things have gone sour, I know you have sinned and I have sinned, I know that these are rough times, but I will remain with you regardless."

Your soft-beating heart under a moonlit sky in Hawaii won't keep you together. The lovely ceremony and the heartfelt vows you spoke are memories you hold dear, but they tend to fade in the harsh light of the world's challenges. It's a decision you make, once for all time, and then confirm with your actions each day. A simple concept that's anything but easy, but no more complicated than deciding to stay.

The following is a letter from a lady who had heard me speak on commitment several years ago. Her words illustrate the simple power of this difficult decision.

I've decided to remain steadfast in commitment to my own marriage that was in the middle of a divorce action. . . . God has changed me. He has given me a new love for my husband and, in turn, my husband has been changing in his attitude toward me. He's still uncommitted about his relationship with Jesus—a miracle I am anticipating.

Six months ago we sat and listened to a non-Christian counselor tell us to get on with the divorce because there was absolutely nothing left in our marriage and no basis upon which to build.

Well, God's grace has allowed the contrary. It's still a real struggle some days, but I've learned that as we "pull" toward each other rather than "push" at each other, the direction is more secure and sound. . . .

So, "commitment" is not just another word in my vocabulary. It's become a real part of my life.

One final "C" in this symphony of survival: Christ. If commitment is the key, then Christ is the lock. I'm amazed that any marriage between nonbelievers lasts very long. Some do last, but I'm always surprised that marriages without Christ don't end sooner. However, if both partners remain steadfastly committed to Christ, regardless, a lasting marriage can become a reality. With His presence in our lives, His transforming power, His constant encouragement, and His infectious compassion steadily working to make us more like Him, how can a marriage fail?

Four

Practical Advice on Making a Marriage Stick

—— ⚭ ——

While I was preaching a series on marriage and the family at Stonebriar Community Church, someone gave me a little sign that reads, "The most difficult years of marriage are those following the wedding."

I was tempted to tape it to the front of the pulpit until we had concluded the series, but I chose not to do that. It occurred to me that people might think I'm more cynical about marriage than I really am. Truth is, the better part of wisdom is knowing how to keep a healthy balance between optimism and cynicism. Remain too optimistic, and eventually your dashed expectations will turn you into a cynic. Indulge your cynicism too long, and you'll lose your sense of humor. Fifty-one years following our wedding, my goal now is to have a reasonably good marriage. I don't expect honeymoon bliss, although we enjoy times that come close. And I won't settle for a perpetual cease-fire, though sometimes that's the best we can do as we get past a disagreement.

Don't be fooled into thinking that once you've made it past a certain milestone you're home free. The effects of Genesis 3 don't dissipate with age, and the temptation to walk away can still overtake you. It's like the joke I heard recently. A woman had been married for seventy years and decided to petition the court for a divorce. The judge asked her, "After all of these years, why?" She answered, "Look, *enough is enough!*"

Our goal is to be more like Mr. and Mrs. Winston Churchill. The British prime minister's razor-sharp wit and tough demeanor had become legendary during the Second World War, almost as much as his tender love for his wife, Clementine. As one story goes, someone asked him, "If you could live your life again, what would you want to be?" After fifty-five years of marriage, Mr. Churchill replied with a twinkle in his eye, "Mrs. Churchill's second husband."

What makes the difference? Some couples would describe their lifetime together as unfulfilling, argumentative, angry, disappointing years. Others having similar circumstances, virtually the same advantages and challenges impacting their marriages, would say, "Our union is solid and satisfying and sure. And it gets better as the years go by." Why? What's the difference?

In the previous chapter, we peeked into the secret lives of three biblical couples. Adam and Eve endured the harsh consequences of sin: banishment from home, cursed ground, cursed relationship, cursed offspring. Yet they remained together through nine hundred years of life. From them we learned that marriage can survive the harshest consequences if the two choose to remain committed.

Then we jumped forward a few hundred years and reviewed the unusual marriage between a prophet and a prostitute. Hosea married Gomer, who may have been a virtuous woman in the beginning but turned out to be grossly unfaithful. Though it came as no surprise, it hurt him nonetheless. After bearing three children, she took to selling her body until it was no good anymore. Then, when Gomer was destitute and sold into slavery, the Lord told Hosea to seek her out, buy her back, and taker her as his wife again. He did that. Hopefully, his life would teach the nation of Israel the depths of God's loyal, persistent, pursuing love for His people—the people who chose spiritual harlotry over the true love of the one true God. And we learned from Hosea and Gomer that a marriage can overcome the most extreme challenges, if they choose commitment over escape.

Then we entered the experience of two remarkable people of faith, Joseph and Mary. He married a virgin, who was carrying a child conceived miraculously from God—a child who is the long-awaited Messiah. Both, having the assurance of truth from heaven, accepted a life of accusation and misunderstanding and a most bizarre set of circumstances in which to make a life together. In spite of the odds against them, their marriage endured; they made a life together, proving that a marriage can endure the strangest circumstances by first choosing commitment.

Commitment is the first necessary ingredient to longevity. But, as we've seen, an enduring marriage isn't necessarily a happy one or even a reasonably good one. So, what's next? To answer that, I want to examine Ephesians 4 (not Ephesians 5, as you might expect). Principles having to do with the role of relationships of men and women in marriage come later. First, we begin with principles that govern our behavior as humans, bearers of God's image, believers in Jesus Christ, members of something greater than ourselves. All of those go together.

I will illustrate some of the principles by unveiling some of the more personal aspects of my own marriage, but certainly not because we have it all together. Not perfectly, anyway. Reasonably well. We have gone through many, if not the same, challenges that you have faced or are currently facing—the same pressures, struggles, heartaches, disappointments, mistakes, and embarrassing failures.

My wife and I are not particularly special in any way. We didn't come from perfect homes or even particularly noteworthy ones in terms of how well they contributed to rearing emotionally healthy children. Our parents were loyal and faithful to each other and to us, but like you, we brought some unhealthy baggage from those families of origin to our marriage. In fact, one of our earliest conversations turned on a shared sense that the Lord would have us rear our children His way, not the way we were reared.

I'm not using our example because we're in Christian ministry either. Rather than helping to make a marriage stronger, being in ministry more likely hinders such from happening. The challenges of ministry are not only unique but have little to offer in terms of helpful advice to strengthen the marriage. Believe me, our ministry-couple experience doesn't give us any supernatural knowledge that isn't already available to you in the pages of your Bible.

No, I use our marriage for two reasons. First, I don't know any other marriage as well as I do ours, or one about which I feel comfortable revealing as much detail. Second, so that you will see that my authority on the subject of marriage doesn't come from fifty-plus years of doing marriage right; my authority comes from Scripture alone. Cynthia and I apply its principles, and we enjoy the benefits of obedience, but we also enjoy the grace of Christ, who keeps us going through the times we fail to practice what we know to be right. We have learned much, but we are continuing to learn—again, just like you.

FIVE PRINCIPLES THAT MAKE A MARRIAGE STICK

In Ephesians 4, I find no fewer than five important principles— mandates, really—that will build on your commitment to marriage and make it stick. Paul originally applied them to the church community, but they work well in many other contexts, especially marriage. Verses 1–24 contain no commands, no imperatives. Then, from verse 25 to the end of the chapter, Paul issues eleven of them! I offer five principles that have helped us maintain a reasonably good marriage . . . so far.

Cultivate Complete Honesty

Therefore, laying aside falsehood, speak truth each one of you with his neighbor, for we are members of one another. (Ephesians 4:25)

Allow me to paraphrase and apply it this way:

[You who are in Christ have been re-created to be living truth.] Therefore, setting aside anything false, each of you speak truth with your married partner, for you are members of one another.

I like Eugene Peterson's rendering:

No more lies, no more pretense. . . . In Christ's body we're all connected to each other, after all. When you lie to others, you end up lying to yourself. (Ephesians 4:25 MSG)

Cynthia and I are learning to cultivate complete honesty in our relationship. Paul says in verse 22, "Lay aside the old self." Then he uses the same word to say, "Lay aside falsehood," or deception. The Greek term translated "falsehood" or "deception" is *pseudos*, from which we get the prefix *pseudo*. A person who is a pseudo-intellectual appears to be a complex thinker when, in truth, he or she may not be very bright at all. The pseudo-intellectual masks his or her real intelligence with deception.

Paul speaks of *pseudos* as though it were an object: "Put it down. Lay it aside." We use *pseudos* as though it were a tool and lying has many variations. It ranges from mild to extreme deception: diplomatic hedging, stretching the facts, not telling the whole story, staying silent when we should speak, whitewashing motives, flattery, twisting the truth, adding false details, contriving stories, embracing fiction as truth.

We reach for *pseudos* in order to fix something in the relationship that we think is broken or might become broken. Unfortunately, it has the very opposite effect. I like the way John R. W. Stott states this. "Fellowship is built on trust, and trust is built on truth. So falsehood undermines fellowship, while truth strengthens it."[1] Change the word "fellowship" to "marriage" and you'll see how well it fits. Marriage is built on trust, and trust is built on truth. *Pseudos* doesn't fix anything. It has the power only to destroy intimacy in a marriage.

I've observed through the years that most of us cultivate the habit of lying while we're dating. We don't just suddenly become liars once we say "I do." For example, a man will commonly tell his wife-to-be how much he loves opera. So he goes to these performances time after time, grinning like a possum eating briar, trying to impress the unsuspecting woman with his love for the arts. She's thinking, *Oh boy, I finally found a man who loves opera as much as I do*! When they return from the honeymoon, he knows he's not going anywhere *near* an opera house again. Why? Because he lied!

Women are just as guilty, only with them it's fishing. A

lovesick woman will get up at three o'clock in the morning, fix those miserable tuna sandwiches, freeze to death on a windy lake, all the while saying, "Oh, this is so much fun. Thanks for taking me." She knows that two seconds after the ceremony will mark her *last* fishing trip! Why did she pretend to like fishing? Because she wanted her husband-to-be to like her.

The truth is hard. It's risky. It requires vulnerability and trust and faith. But some couples have covered themselves with fig leaves for so long, they can hardly stand the thought of being naked in front of each other. They've hidden behind deception so long, they can barely recognize the truth. How sad to live in such a trap.

If the truth sets us free, then no marriage is more in bondage than a marriage that's wrapped in *pseudos*—deception, untruth, lies. Lay it aside and determine *today* to begin speaking only truth. I would suggest starting by admitting the truth about yourself.

Express Anger in Appropriate Ways and at the Right Time

> Be angry, and yet do not sin; do not let the sun go down on your anger, and do not give the devil an opportunity. (Ephesians 4:26–27)

Go ahead and be angry. You do well to be angry—but don't use your anger as fuel for revenge. And don't stay angry. Don't go to bed angry. Don't give the Devil that kind of foothold in your life. (Ephesians 4:26–27 MSG)

Cynthia and I are learning to express our anger in appropriate ways and at the right time. Please notice I did not say, "We are learning never to be angry." Scripture says we're supposed to be angry. The Greek verb is a command, which is actually a little softer than the Hebrew of Psalm 4:4, which reads, "Tremble, and do not sin." Not only is it OK to be angry, the Bible says, in effect, "Go ahead and shake with red-faced rage if you need to . . . but sinning is off-limits."

Perhaps, like me, you were reared to believe that anger is always sinful. For ten years, I criticized Cynthia anytime I saw anger cross her face. But I was wrong. Not all anger is bad. We should be angry to see the innocent defrauded or good values punished. We should tremble with rage when we see or even hear of a child beaten. Let me add, if you can watch a newscast that reports a child molestation and it doesn't make your blood boil, something is terribly wrong! And shrugging off a serious offense by your closest, most trusted companion—your mate—is a sure sign that the two of you are disconnected.

Not only is anger not, in itself, sinful, but righteous anger reflects the mind of God. Take note of God's reaction to deception in particular:

> Let no one deceive you with empty words, for because of these things the wrath of God comes upon the sons of disobedience. (Ephesians 5:6)

If all anger were sinful, God would be wrong to be angry toward the sons of disobedience. Furthermore, the psalms are teeming with this kind of writing. When confronted with sin, the Lord is anything but tolerant, passive, or apathetic. And we do well to follow His example. The anger we feel is very often appropriate to the situation. Unfortunately, we just as often express that anger in immature or sinful ways. To be like Him, we must learn to express it appropriately and at the right time.

Appropriate expression of anger never causes fear, never belittles or intimidates, and never shuts another person down. On the other hand, we can't become suddenly fragile, distant, or condescending to our partners when they begin to vent. A marriage characterized by mutual respect will allow each partner enough room to express angry feelings. And, in my experience, managing angry expression requires teamwork. The angry partner must exercise self-control ("do not sin"), while the other partner responds to angry expressions appropriately. The quickest way to calm an angry mate is to listen. Work hard to hear what your partner is expressing (however poorly) and show empathy.

Timely expression of anger also requires teamwork. Keep short accounts. Paul's instruction includes the command, "Do not let the sun go down on your anger."

Cynthia suggested years ago that we should never go to bed angry. She wisely noted, "When we do, it's like wet cement that will harden during the night." So we stay up until the conflict has been resolved. Of course, by about three thirty in the morning, you'll agree to just about anything. But, even if one of you has to "lose" the argument, it's better than going to bed back to back. Time can become your enemy, giving your anger a place to fester, which brings us to the intriguing phrase, "and do not give the devil an opportunity."

The word translated "opportunity" is the Greek word *topos*, which simply means place. But this is one of those loaded words that carries with it a whole realm of associated meanings. Figuratively it can mean opportunity, sanctuary, or territory, but I find the Hebrew Old Testament usage the most intriguing. They used the word "place" to refer to holy places or hallowed ground where a god was worshiped. The New Testament used *topos* to refer to an office of authority in government or the church. Paul and his audience knew all of these meanings, and I think he intended all of them to apply here. I would paraphrase it this way:

Do not erect a shrine to your anger in your heart.
The devil will appoint himself its priest.

Perhaps you have done just that. Rather than face your mate with your anger, clearly expressing how he or she caused you pain, you have nurtured the offense. You stored it neatly away and convinced yourself that you are "letting it go." But you occasionally take it out and caress the offense, remembering how wrong your mate was and how right you are. You might even have more than one offense. You may have a large mental storage room for collected hurts and injustices. Funny how they get bigger in there when you're not looking. Truth gets twisted, facts are distorted, and small things become bloated.

What are you waiting for? Surely, you're not holding out until the right time to unload them on your partner all at once, are you? The longer you wait, the greater opportunity you give Satan to invade, to weaken, and ultimately to break your marriage into splintered pieces. If you have allowed them to collect over time, don't expect a quick resolution. They will have to come out as slowly as you put them in. And you may need a competent counselor to help you clean out that closet appropriately and completely . . . at the right time.

Don't Steal from Your Mate

> He who steals must steal no longer; but rather he must labor, performing with his own hands what is good, so that he will have something to share with one who has need. (Ephesians 4:28)

Cynthia and I have learned to stop stealing from each other. (That will raise a few eyebrows!)

Paul's concern was not robbery, and I doubt that he meant "stealing" in the sense of one person pilfering from another's home. According to one fine dictionary, the term means "to steal, secretly and craftily to embezzle and appropriate."[2] Paul wrote this to a church with its share of freeloaders. Anyone who claims to be a part of the community, enjoying the fruit of its labor, yet contributes nothing is stealing. So is the one who withholds gifts or time or labor or involvement. To share in the community is to contribute a fair share of hard work. I can think of no better cure for stealing than hard labor, either voluntary in good faith or involuntary behind bars.

So how does this apply to marriage? A marriage involves more than material possessions. It's a community of two, each having exchanged promises and expectations. My time, my trust, my work, my best self, even my body belongs in part to Cynthia. When I withhold or violate any of those things, I rob Cynthia of what is rightfully hers.

I steal when I let something else encroach on the time I promised her. I steal when I give my very best at the church and leave nothing for her at home. I steal when I reveal something she asked me to hold in confidence. I steal when she entrusts me with a vulnerability, and I use it against her. I steal when she confesses a sin, and I hold it against her.

Couples steal from each other by using household money selfishly. I know of one example where the husband loved the game of golf and played two or three times a week. There's nothing particularly wrong with that except that he was also tightfisted with his wife at home. He'd throw a fit if she went over the budget at the grocery store, and she had to be very careful buying clothes. Eventually, she reached her limit. She calmly sat him down and said, "I'm going to start keeping track of how much you spend at the golf course, then I'm spending the same amount at Nordstrom. Play as many rounds as you want."

It's amazing what that did to curb his golf habit! Unfortunately, stealing was only one problem in that marriage. And it eventually came apart.

Guard those things in a marriage that belong to your mate. Keep them safe and use them wisely. A good example is your time. Cynthia and I have observed that unless we write down appointments—schedule time and protect it as we would a crucial meeting—other duties will creep in like a thief and rob us of time alone. When we write down that time in an appointment calendar, it's more difficult to steal it back unwittingly.

Closely Guard Your Speech

> Let no unwholesome word proceed from your mouth, but only such a word as is good for edification according to the need of the moment, so that it will give grace to those who hear. And do not grieve the Holy Spirit of God, with whom you were sealed for the day of redemption. (Ephesians 4:29–30)

Washington Irving put it very well: "The tongue is the only tool that grows sharper with constant use." Sharp instruments can be deadly when handled carelessly and yet extremely useful in the hands of a skilled surgeon. Wisdom makes all the difference.

The Greek sentence is a little awkward, but it drives the point home: "Every putrid word from your mouth, let it not depart." I like the odd way that is expressed. It is often translated "Let no unwholesome word proceed from your mouth," which is a fine rendering. But the literal Greek assumes that the words already exist and that we have a choice as to what will happen to them. The original language states it as we experience it. Words come to mind, and our responsibility is to evaluate them before speaking them.

The word "unwholesome" is too mild. The Greek term refers to rotting vegetables or rancid fish. This reminds me of a practical joke we used to play on newlyweds when I was a teenager growing up in muggy Houston. While the happy couple enjoyed their reception, a few of us boys would load the hubcaps of the getaway car with raw shrimp. Maybe a few placed lovingly on the engine block for good measure. After about three or four days in the Houston heat, "unwholesome" would have been too mild to describe the stench surrounding that car. The slimy, gray ooze slinging from the hubcaps is what Paul considers speech that doesn't give grace to others.

Cynthia has placed a copy of this verse out of the Amplified Bible at the top of her computer screen.

Whenever she sits to send an e-mail, these words remind her that the keyboard can be just as powerful as the tongue.

Cynthia and I are learning over the years to be very careful with our words and even the tone of our words. Your tongue can be a devastating weapon in your home. You can do everything else right. You can be a mature husband or wife. You can be the fulfillment of your mate's every dream. Nevertheless, all of that can be undone—completely nullified—by the words you speak and the manner in which you speak them.

Each time we open our mouths we either build up or tear down our mates. We either affirm or assault. Few things can be divided so neatly into the categories of "edifying" and "putrid," but our speech is one of them. Strangely enough, we are more careful to speak nicely to people in public than we are with our own spouses. How sad for us, and how it grieves the Holy Spirit to witness it.

Be Nice

Let all bitterness and wrath and anger and clamor and slander be put away from you, along with all malice. Be kind to one another, tender-hearted, forgiving each other, just as God in Christ also has forgiven you. (Ephesians 4:31–32)

My sister, Luci, paraphrases all those words this way: "Just be nice." I like that. It boils down this command to something very simple without trivializing the passage. "Nice" is something everyone can do. Courtesy is woven into the fabric of "nice." You do it in public to total strangers every day. You set aside your bad mood and your worries just long enough to return a smile, offer a compliment, absorb a cross word, or offer assistance.

"Nice" is helpful in another respect. It's simple. When men think of ways to show love to their wives, we tend to think of grand gestures like jewelry and trips to exotic places. Perhaps thinking that nothing else is quite good enough, we hold back doing the small things. Yet for women, the smallest kindnesses mean so much.

I once got a rush of affection for Cynthia, so I pulled off a Post-It note (wouldn't want to spend too much, you know) and wrote the three words: "I love you." I stuck it on her mirror and took off for the office. When I came home later it was gone and I didn't think much more about it. I figured she saw it, smiled, wadded it up, and went about her day. But to my surprise, we took a drive in her car a few evenings later and there it was, stuck to her dashboard. Three simple words, but they meant the world to her. (She kept the note there for weeks.)

I smiled, we kissed, and then a little light bulb flickered on in my head. I was amazed. That's all it takes to make her feel loved and appreciated and affirmed? Most times, yes. Simple, authentic gestures of affection laid end to end, day by day over the years will give her more affirmation than a dozen trips to Tahiti and half the diamonds in South Africa.

Women, too, have their lessons to learn. Criticism chips away at a man's dignity and leaves him with less strength to love his wife. Ladies, be nice to your husband by finding something that he does that pleases you. Point it out and thank him for being a good husband. Even better, notice something in his character that you admire, then tell him that you respect him for it. (To men, love and respect are the same.) I think you will be as amazed as I was at how something so simple will take your husband so far.

That's how people are transformed. That's how we bring out the very best in our married partners. Just be nice.

The kindness of Scottish pastor and author Alexander Whyte is legendary. It was said of him, "All Whyte's geese are swans." I love that line! His parishioners became swans because he saw them that way. What is your husband becoming because of you? Is your wife becoming a more fulfilled person by your kindness?

A Picture of the Grace-Filled Marriage

Ultimately, this passage is calling for us to exercise grace in our relationships, and I am calling particular attention to the marriage relationship. Cultivate complete honesty, express your anger appropriately and at the right time, don't steal from each other, guard your speech, and find ways to show kindness to each other. Just think how easy remaining committed would be, how natural and deep intimacy would become, if you and your partner in life obeyed these five, simple mandates each day.

Allow me to close this chapter with a final illustration of grace at work in a marriage. This true story comes from a poignant book by Richard Selzer, MD titled *Mortal Lessons: Notes in the Art of Surgery*:

> I stand by the bed where a young woman lies, her face postoperative, her mouth twisted in palsy, clownish. A tiny twig of the facial nerve, the one to the muscles of her mouth, has been severed. She will be thus from now on. The surgeon had followed with religious fervor the curve of her flesh; I promise you that. Nevertheless, to remove the tumor in her cheek, I had to cut the little nerve.
>
> Her young husband is in the room. He stands on

the opposite side of the bed, and together they seem to dwell in the evening lamplight, isolated from me, private. Who are they, I ask myself, he and this wry-mouth I have made, who gaze at and touch each other so generously, greedily? The young woman speaks.

"Will my mouth always be like this?" she asks.

"Yes," I say, "it will. It's because the nerve was cut."

She nods and is silent. But the young man smiles.

"I like it," he says. "It is kind of cute."

All at once I *know* who he is. I understand, and I lower my gaze. One is not bold in an encounter with a god. Unmindful, he bends to kiss her crooked mouth, and I'm so close I can see how he twists his own lips to accommodate to hers, to show her that their kiss still works. I remember that the gods appeared in ancient Greece as mortals, and I hold my breath and let the wonder in.[3]

Grace. It's oxygen to a marriage and far too many are gasping for it. Breathe life into yours with these five principles. Take them seriously and apply them in whatever unique ways fit your mate. Apply the same diligence and creativity to your marriage you would give an assignment at work. Your reward will not only be a long, stable union, but a happy, fulfilling one as well.

Five

Essential Glue for Every Couple to Apply

———— ⚭ ————

Love—genuine love—is something that defies definition. For millennia, words have eluded the very best poets and philosophers in their quest to analyze love, quantify love, explain love, or define love. But where words leave the brain numb, the heart resonates in perfect pitch when we see love in action. Join me as we look in on some familiar scenes.

We're in a busy airport. An announcement over the intercom stirs a small commotion behind us as a man in uniform stands up. Tiny arms encircle each leg as an elderly couple looks on, weeping. He and his wife cling to each other in a long, desperate embrace. Tears and kisses and prayers and promises lead up to the inevitable "I love you . . . goodbye"—perhaps to be their last.

We're strolling down a dimly lit hospital hallway at three a.m. when the squeaks and coos of a nursing new-born draw our attention. There, in an island of soft light, is a new mother cradling the life that came from her body only hours before. Her husband sits behind her on the bed, his cheek pressed against hers as they stare in wonder at their baby. The expression on their faces reflects the miracle that has just occurred: love begat life.

The smell of fresh flowers and the jubilant chords of a pipe organ mingle together over our heads in a church sanctuary. A bride moves gracefully down the aisle, holding her father's arm. He wears the look of a man who's about to hand a million-dollar Stradivarius to a gorilla.[1] At the altar, a young man stands on tiptoe, peering down the aisle for a glimpse of his bride. On his face we see innocence, fear, anticipation, delight, and enormous love.

Love never shines brighter than when displayed against the utter blackness of death. Patrick Morley tells this true story in his book *The Man in the Mirror*:

The salmon nearly leaped onto their hooks! That was a far cry from the day before when the four anglers couldn't even seem to catch an old boot.

Disappointed but not discouraged, they had climbed aboard their small seaplane and skimmed over the Alaskan mountains to a pristine, secluded bay where the fish were sure to bite.

They parked their aircraft and waded upstream, where the water teemed with ready-to-catch salmon. Later that afternoon, when they returned to their camp, they were surprised to find the seaplane high and dry. The tides fluctuated twenty-three feet in that particular bay, and the pontoons rested on a bed of gravel. Since they couldn't fly out till morning, they settled in for the night and enjoyed some of their catch for dinner, then slept in the plane.

In the morning the seaplane was adrift, so they promptly cranked the engine and started to take off. Too late, they discovered one of the pontoons had been punctured and was filled with water. The extra weight threw the plane into a circular pattern. Within moments from liftoff the seaplane careened into the sea and capsized.

Dr. Phil Littleford determined that everyone was alive, including his twelve-year-old son, Mark. He suggested that they pray, which the other two men quickly endorsed. No safety equipment could be found on board—no life vests, no flares, nothing. The plane gurgled and submerged into the blackness of the icy morning sea. The frigid Alaskan water chilled their breath.

They all began to swim for shore, but the rip-tide

countered every stroke. The two men alongside Phil and Mark were strong swimmers and they both made shore, one just catching the tip of land as the tides pulled them out toward sea.

Their two companions last saw Phil and Mark as a disappearing dot on the horizon, swept arm-in-arm out to sea.

The Coast Guard reported they probably lasted no more than an hour in the freezing waters—hypothermia would chill the body functions and they would go to sleep. Mark, with a smaller body mass, would fall asleep first in his father's arms. Phil could have made the shoreline, too, but that would have meant abandoning his son. Their bodies were never found.[2]

LOVE ON DISPLAY

When we see love in action, our hearts cannot help but beat in perfect rhythm with those involved. Love is a universal language. When expressed authentically, no words are necessary. Furthermore, love is no less essential to human life than air, food, or water. Hard science proves the fact. And, as we'll see in the apostle Paul's towering treatise in 1 Corinthians 13, nothing is complete without love. Unfortunately, we love too little and we love too seldom. So, on occasion, we need a gentle reminder of what it means to love others with our whole hearts. That calls for wisdom and counsel from the Author of love.

In my earlier chapters, I underscored the importance of commitment. We discovered five commands in Ephesians 4 that will add sweetness to longevity, so that an enduring marriage can also be an enjoyable one. But let's face it. A marriage without love makes no sense. It's like a concert without music.

Imagine. The performers work to gain mastery of their instruments. The conductor selects a musical composition. A grand music hall is rented, programs printed, and a date set. People from all over the city and beyond, dressed in their finest evening attire, file into the decorated hall at the appointed time and take their seats. First-chair oboe tunes the rest of the orchestra so that every instrument resonates in perfect, harmonious pitch. The conductor appears, bows, mounts the platform, and then . . . nothing. Silence. The musicians leave their instruments either on their laps or placed beside them on the floor. The audience sits in orderly stillness. Then, after an hour or so, the conductor faces the audience and takes a bow, which prompts their applause. He motions to the orchestra, and the audience continues to clap and whistle. He exits the stage as the ovation gives way to murmuring voices and shuffling feet as the audience empties the hall.

Absurd? Yes. But so are too many marriages today. Committed, civil, pleasant, but empty of the very thing marriage was designed to display: love. Commitment will keep you and your partner sitting side by side, but love is what bonds you. Merriam-Webster adds these synonyms to the definition for married: *united, joined.* Love is the glue that unites two lives, joining together two committed partners into an unbreakable union.

Most of the essentials of love can be found in the first half of 1 Corinthians 13, Paul's grand discourse on love. As we examine this well-known passage, I fear that familiarity will obscure the genius it contains. Looking at something familiar from a fresh perspective requires mental discipline. So I ask, if this is not your first exposure to these verses, please pretend that it is. Determine to take Paul's words very personally. Let them slowly seep into your mind and then allow them to impact you.

THE PRIORITY OF LOVE

Paul begins his treatise with three statements, emphasizing the priority of love.

> If I speak with the tongues of men and of angels, but do not have love, I have become a noisy gong or a clanging cymbal. If I have the gift of prophecy, and

know all mysteries and all knowledge; and if I have all faith, so as to remove mountains, but do not have love, I am nothing. And if I give all my possessions to feed the poor, and if I surrender my body to be burned, but do not have love, it profits me nothing. (1 Corinthians 13:1–3)

What amazing analogies! His first statement measures the importance of love against the gift of communication. If any of us knew the language of those mysterious, heavenly creatures that fill the throne room of God, or if we possessed the skill to capture the attention of audiences with our words and hold them spellbound with our eloquence yet at the same time lacked love, our words would be pointless, meaningless, and profitless. Without love, we have nothing of value to say. No amount of oratory giftedness or linguistic skill can substitute for love. Our mouth moves as sounds emerge, but everything falls flat if love is missing.

Ephesians 4:14–15 encourages us to speak the truth in love. Truth without love is cruel at worst, empty at best. If I confront someone with words and I don't do it because of love, I shouldn't be surprised to find them injured rather than healed. Loveless confrontation helps no one. If I attempt to comfort someone in pain without love as my motivation, my words will cause more sorrow than if I had just stayed away. Empty consolation fools no one. And if I try to instruct people without love as my guide, they will resist any application of the principles, however valid. They would only hear me for what I am: a heady, self-important, intellectual snob. Academic instruction changes no one.

Paul's second statement measures the value of love against spiritual giftedness and maturity. Take note of the spiritual gifts and skills he mentions:

Prophecy, the ability to speak the words and predict the works of God

Omniscience, complete knowledge of all things, including the mind of God

Faith, such oneness with God as to accomplish the physically impossible

If we had that kind of spiritual maturity, we would be like Christ, wouldn't we? We may wield the powers of almighty God, yet if we didn't possess His uniquely defining quality of love, we are nothing. Think of it—*nothing*!

Then, perhaps thinking of Christ's gift to us, Paul's third statement measures love against sacrificial living and martyrdom. Selflessness that feeds the hungry, houses the homeless, cares for the sick, advances a great cause, even selflessness to the point of death accomplishes nothing if it lacks love. Remember the moving story of Dr. Phil Littleford and his son, Mark? Remove love from that story and what remains? Vanity, foolishness, something so strange we can't even identify with it.

THE SPECIAL NATURE OF *AGAPE*

The word Paul uses no fewer than nine times in this chapter is *agape*—rarely found outside the Bible—probably because the meaning is unique to the kind of love we experience with God. The Greek had *eros*, an intoxicating, impulsive love between men and women; and *philos*, the warm, noble affection of deep friendship. But *agape* was a seldom used and poorly understood term. The scholarly *Theological Dictionary of the New Testament* contrasts the meaning of *eros* and *agape* this way:

Eros	Agape
• a general love of the world seeking satisfaction wherever it can.	• a love which makes distinctions, choosing and keeping to its object.
• determined by a more or less indefinite impulsion towards its object [him or her].	• a free and decisive act determined by its subject [us].

Eros	Agape
• in its highest sense is used of the upward impulsion of man, of his love for the divine.	• relates for the most part the love of God, to the love of the higher lifting up the lower, elevating the lower above others.
• seeks in others the fulfillment of its own life's hunger.	• must often be translated "to show love"; it is a giving, active love on the other's behalf.[3]

Few put it better than Dr. Ron Allen in his footnote in the *Nelson Study Bible*:

This word, *agape,* describes a love that is based on the deliberate choice of the one who loves rather than the worthiness of the one who is loved. This kind of love goes against natural human inclination. It is a giving, selfless, expect-nothing-in-return kind of love. . . .

Our modern "throw-away" society encourages us to get rid of people in our lives who are difficult to get along with, whether they are friends, family, or acquaintances. Yet this attitude runs in complete contrast to the love described by Paul. True love puts up with people who would be easier to give up on.[4]

LOVE IN ACTION

Every marriage needs a healthy dose of *eros*—a passionate, emotional, lusty appetite for each other. But that's not the kind of love that holds a couple together . . . for the long haul. Where *eros* is a mystery that evokes good feelings, *agape* is a choice that reveals good character. In 1 Corinthians 13: 4–7, Paul gives us more than a dozen characteristics of *agape*, the essential glue every married couple needs.

Some of the characteristics are described positively ("love is . . ."), while most are expressed negatively ("love is not . . ."). Each description is worth noting on its own as you evaluate the strength and quality of your love for your spouse. As we look at them, I challenge you to ask yourself two questions with each characteristic. First, "How am I doing in this area?" Second, "How would my partner's behavior change if my love included this?"

Love Is Patient and Kind (v. 4)

In English, we use the term "short-tempered" to describe someone who is easily angered or has a volatile personality. You never know what will set this person off. The Greek term is the compound of two words. The first is *thymia*.

We get our word *thermometer* from this ancient term. It has in mind the idea of heat or, in this case, passion or anger. The second is *macro*, the opposite of *micro*. Love is "long-tempered." Love has a long fuse. One writer describes *macrothymia* as "the capacity to be wronged and not retaliate."[5] Love is patient. How are you doing with patience? How would your spouse's behavior change if your love were more patient?

Love is also kind. In our rapid-fire era, we've forgotten how to be kind. Jesus used a form of this word to describe wine that has aged and mellowed (Luke 5:38–39) and to describe a disciple's service to Him. He said,

> Come to Me, all who are weary and heavy-laden, and I will give you rest. Take My yoke upon you and learn from Me, for I am gentle and humble in heart, and you will find rest for your souls. For My yoke is easy and My burden is light. (Matthew 11:28–30)

Paul's word to describe love derives from the word Jesus used, translated "easy" in this passage. This quality of love is "serviceable," "useful," "adapted to its purpose," "good, of its kind."[6] A. T. Robertson called it "gentle in behavior." This is not a theological word, but it is a Jesus kind of love.

Think of a person who is mellow, not easily ruffled,

someone who is both strong and gentle. Aren't people like that enjoyable to be around? You feel safe and relaxed in their presence. They have a love that is patient and kind.

Love Is Not Jealous or Arrogant (v. 4)

Think of these two terms in contrast to "patient and kind."

First, love is not jealous. Few things turn off a mate faster than a suspicious, insecure, smothering protectiveness. A jealous lover's first concern is for self, which is the exact opposite of *agape*. Rather than being patient, the jealous lover zealously pursues what he or she wants, even to the extreme of controlling someone else.

Second, love does not brag, which is the chief occupation of the arrogant. An arrogant person has one exclusive concern: self. Paul selected a particular Greek word that sounds like what it is. The word is *phusio*, pronounced fffffoooooooo-zee-o. It means "to blow, to puff up, to inflate." The verb comes from a noun meaning "bellows." Years ago, every fireplace had an accordion-like contraption next to it. If the fire decreased to embers, someone would grab the bellows, pull the handles apart so it would fill with air, then quickly squeeze. The result was a long blast of air that would fan the dying coals into a flame again.

We've all been around someone like that. The handles

pull apart as he or she puffs up, then the handles squeeze and out comes a long blast of *meeeeeeeeeee*. You may have noticed that it never inspires admiration. If anything, the arrogant blowhard only draws more criticism. Like the mother whale warning her young, "Don't go up there and blow so hard. That's when you get harpooned!"

On the other hand, how pleasant and surprising it is to be around individuals who are well known, gifted, and sought after, but who never make demands or expect special treatment. Cynthia and I have a longtime friend who left his former career to work as a business manager for a small Bible college. As Joe got underway in that job, he and the leadership of that school decided that a good athletic program would help put the institution on the map. Football required far more money than they could invest, so they chose basketball. The Lord seemed to affirm that decision by sending—virtually out of the blue—a Christian man who also happened to be a very gifted coach. Recruiting top-notch players without the clout of a big-name school or money for scholarships would be their next challenge.

One day, the phone rang and a voice on the other end said, "I understand you're the business manager. We've never met. My name is John."

After a polite exchange, the man continued, "I've followed basketball for a long time, and I hear you'd like to get a team going. I think that's wonderful. I love your school and I've watched it grow from almost nothing. As a matter of fact, I know your new coach, and I also know a very gifted kid he'd like to meet. He could easily become an All-American, in my opinion, but for some reason recruiters have overlooked him. I could arrange a meeting if you would like that."

Of course, Joe agreed. They ended up recruiting the young man along with two of his friends. That combination gave them a winning squad almost immediately. Some time later Joe began to wonder who John was. His call had made everything possible. So he did some digging only to discover that John, who called him, was John Wooden, the six-time NCAA Coach of the Year for the UCLA Bruins who took his teams to ten national championship victories in twelve seasons! His introduction? "Hi, I'm John. I've followed basketball for a long time."

Keep in mind, *agape* is a humble love. If we love our mates with this kind of love, we will be more concerned with serving and helping him or her rather than inflating ourselves. Love isn't arrogant.

Love Is Charming (v. 5)

Paul says, "[Love] does not act unbecomingly; it does not seek its own." The word "unbecoming" describes someone who is rude or crude, someone without class or decorum. In the positive sense, love is tactful, courteous—I would use the word "charming." Merriam-Webster defines *charming* as "extremely pleasing or delightful."[7]

Charming love brings out the best in other people. Howie Stevenson, our minister of worship for many years in the church I served in Fullerton, California, taught me that people are charmed into righteousness. I've never heard anyone say, "You know what? He slammed me over the head with a baseball bat, and I realized I need to be more like Christ" or, "She treated me like dirt, and now I want to see things her way and follow Jesus." Of course not! The kind of love that bonds people is a winsome, charming love that thinks more of others than of self.

This is important because we often want the person we love to behave in a certain way, which then influences how we behave toward him or her. This is the very self-serving attitude that Paul warns against with the words "love does not seek its own." Love for our mates will seek to bring out the best in them by giving without conditions or expectations.

Love Has a Thick Skin (v. 5)

Paul uses two negative descriptions—"is not provoked" and "doesn't take into account a wrong suffered." In other words, genuine love isn't fragile. *Agape* applies lots of grace to a relationship; it leaves lots of room for the other person to make mistakes. And when you live in close proximity to someone for the majority of a lifetime, there will be lots of them to overlook.

I've seen both men and women who are constantly irritated by their mates. The smallest error—a wrong look, a misplaced word, a simple oversight—causes miniature explosions throughout the day. These little outbursts of irritability must certainly be the result of keeping a long list of wrongs close at hand. Paul uses an accounting term to caution us against keeping a mental ledger of bad deeds. When we do that, we're the losers. Warren Wiersbe writes:

> One of the most miserable men I ever met was a professed Christian who actually kept in a notebook a list of the wrongs he felt others had committed against him. Forgiveness means that we wipe the record clean and never hold things against people.[8]

The truth is, we can keep a list without writing anything down or even realizing it. If you find that your mate irritates you for reasons that you must admit are minor, the chances are good that he or she has something on the wrong side of your ledger sheet. Either address your anger appropriately and promptly, or simply let it go.

Love Loves Truth (v. 6)

Paul then combines a negative with a positive statement to describe the role of truth in a love relationship. Let me caution you: the implications of this powerful statement run deep.

> [Love] does not rejoice in unrighteousness, but rejoices with the truth. (1 Corinthians 13:6)

For Paul, *agape* is the intersection of truth, salvation, and obedience to God. And this is where your marriage and Christ meet.

Stop. Read that again slowly and, preferably, aloud.

Your love for your mate should encourage his or her love relationship with the Lord. Righteousness is a shared goal because individually it is your highest calling as a believer. You are both pursuing the same truth because the Author of truth called you to Himself. He's also the One who gave you each other as a helper in life's journey. That's why love and truth have been inseparable companions since before time. They *always* go together. Where you find love, you find truth. And when you seek the highest good of another, truth is absolutely essential.

Sometimes, as a lover of your mate, you must tell him or her the truth, even though that truth is not pleasant. The truth may be something difficult to hear about yourself, which will require all the courage you can gather. Your trust will be put to the test. Your partner may fail to respond with grace. But to enjoy an authentic relationship, your love must be based upon truth.

Sometimes, the truth will be something about your mate that he or she may find difficult to hear. If you are eager to reveal it, I suggest you wait. If you are reluctant, you are probably in the best position to apply the needed tact and gentleness to help your mate discover a difficult truth. When telling the truth in love, the sole motivation is the good of the other person, which means your speech will be laced with patience and kindness.

Where there is love, there is transparent and unguarded honesty, even when the honesty is not easy to express.

The Limits of Love (v. 7)

For Paul, *agape* has limits like the universe has edges. He measures the dimensions of love in four directions: patience, trust, confidence, and endurance. Observe how he weaves the four threads together, forming a tapestry of love.

[Love] bears all things, believes all things, hopes all things, endures all things. (1 Corinthians 13:7)

Your love shelters the relationship from anything that should fall upon it. Your love chooses to trust your mate and believes the best of him or her in the midst of challenging circumstances. Your love expresses confidence in the faithfulness and goodness of your spouse despite how hopeless things may seem. And your love chooses to remain steadfast, opting for a long-term view through short-term difficulties. The insightful British commentator Alfred Plummer summarized this verse well when he wrote, "When love has no evidence, it believes the best. When the evidence is adverse, it hopes for the best. And when hopes are repeatedly disappointed, it still courageously waits."[9]

APPLYING THE GLUE

Love, like glue, has the potential to create a bond, but only when released from its container. If you want something to stick, you have to apply it. Authentic love is demonstrative. What we have discovered so far is convicting enough; so let me keep this simple with three short phrases. These are merely a place to start.

Write It Down

Express your love in writing. A computer printout or an e-mail is a nice, everyday expression, and I certainly encourage you to do that. But, on occasion, express your love in your own handwriting. Take some time to think about your mate and why you love him or her, then hand-write your note or a brief letter. Too often we walk around with thoughts that, for some reason, never find expression. Yet the impact of those thoughts—however poorly put into words—can be amazing.

I was in the home of some friends when I happened to walk up the stairs. As I neared the top, I noticed something familiar hanging in the hallway: my handwriting! I had written a simple note to thank them for something and express how much I loved them . . . and to my surprise, they actually framed it! Now that couple hears me thank and affirm them every time they walk up the stairs.

Something else occurs when I take the time to write out my thoughts by hand. As I write the note, I remember all over again how much I love Cynthia, and all the things I appreciate about her, and why I always want to be with her. As I am reminded, she is reminded, and the experience stirs up all of those wonderful "in love" emotions that deepen and enrich a marriage.

Most likely, this habit will not come naturally to you. That's OK. It doesn't for most of us, myself included. This is *agape*, love that arises from the seat of your will not the seat of your emotions. Give your love tangible expression. Handwritten notes are a wonderful way to start. And so . . . *write it down.*

Risk It Often

I know this can be a tough one for some. You may have a long history of people taking advantage of your good nature and stepping on your heart. Perhaps the idea of being vulnerable enough to love without reservation feels too risky for you. Unfortunately, you have no alternative. Love and risk cannot be separated. C. S. Lewis wrote some of his most memorable words on the subject of love in his work *The Four Loves.*

> To love at all is to be vulnerable. Love anything, and your heart will certainly be wrung and possibly broken. If you want to make sure of keeping it intact, you must give your heart to no one, not even to an animal. Wrap it carefully round with hobbies and little luxuries; avoid all entanglements; lock it safe in the casket or the coffin of your selfishness. But in that casket—safe, dark, motionless, airless—it will

change. It will not be broken; it will become unbreakable, impenetrable, irredeemable. The alternative to tragedy, or at least to the risk of tragedy, is damnation. The only place outside Heaven where you can be perfectly safe from all the dangers and perturbations of love is Hell.[10]

Risk loving your mate without reservation or qualification or condition. You have survived being hurt in the past, and the Lord will not allow you to suffer more than you can manage. Pain is likely if you choose to love, but a living death is certain if you don't. So, you see? You really don't have any other alternative. Risk it. *Risk it often.*

Do It Now

It's easy to substitute life for work and pat ourselves on the back—that is, until something threatens our lives. After Senator Paul Tsongas was diagnosed with cancer, a friend wrote to him, affirming his decision not to run for re-election. We would do well to remember his sobering words: "No man ever said on his deathbed, 'I wish I had spent more time in the office.'"[11]

Don't wait until tomorrow. Satan would love to lull you into a procrastinating complacency that always believes there will be time enough tomorrow, or next week, or once the big project is done, or after things settle down just a little, or . . . or . . . or . . . Trust me, having lived for more than seventy years—fifty-one of them married—there will *never* come a convenient time to love your mate the way 1 Corinthians 13 describes.

So, *do it now.* Don't wait for the atmospheric conditions to be right, don't expect that with less stress it will come naturally, don't hope that it will take care of itself once this or that is resolved. As my friends at the Minirth Clinic like to say, "Love is a choice."

Choose to love your mate *now.*

You probably will never find yourself floating in icy waters, clinging to someone you adore, facing the question, "Do I push away and save myself, or do I choose to love?" No, in small ways, a dozen times a day, you answer that question. Your next opportunity is coming soon. Be on the lookout for it. Then write it . . . risk it . . . do it.

Six

What Families Need to Thrive

When Edith Schaeffer, wife of the late philosopher and theologian Francis Schaeffer, decided to write her book on the home, she chose a title that asked the question, *What Is a Family?* Each of her chapter titles proposed an answer. Some of them are, "The Birthplace of Creativity," "A Shelter in the Time of Storm," "A Perpetual Relay of Truth," "An Educational Control," and my favorite, "A Museum of Memories."

Let me ask you, as you stroll the halls of your museum of memories, what do you see? Beauty? Sadness? Do the exhibits recall mostly episodes of pain, mistreatment, perhaps even neglect or abuse? Maybe you see mostly recollections of laughter and artifacts from a joyous, delightful childhood. Take a few moments now to revisit your memory. Do it now. This could be important.

Carlos Baker, in his biography of Ernest Hemingway,

notes that the legendary author struggled with anger, bouts of depression, and alcoholism. In his later years, Hemingway became more vulnerable regarding the truth of the "black rage" he often felt for his father. According to Baker,

> Ernest mentioned the small shed for garden tools in the back yard at Windemere. It commanded a view of the path into which Dr. Hemingway sometimes stepped while working among his tomato vines. Ernest reported that when his father had punished him and he was angry, he had sometimes sat in the open door of the shed with his shotgun, drawing a bead on his father's head.[1]

Ironically, it was a shotgun that Ernest Hemingway used to take his own life during the sustained delusion of his final days. What dark memories he had!

On the other hand, Corrie ten Boom was shaped by good memories of her "papa." Every night as she crawled into bed, he placed a hand on her head and prayed for her, always ending their time together with the words, "Corrie, I love you." She said that even the horrors of the concentration camp at Ravensbruck could not erase those memories. Sometimes closing her eyes at night would be difficult, having seen suffering and death all day. But she found peace by imagining her heavenly Father's hand on her head saying to her, "Corrie, I love you."

Memories are more than images stored in the attic or basement of your mind. They are part of the building material from which you are constructed. They are the pattern after which you will unconsciously construct your new home—*your* marriage, *your* family. And nothing has a greater influence on you than how you regard those memories, how you arrange them and interpret them, how you allow them to influence you consciously and even unconsciously.

This is a book about marriage, but not merely so. My overall concern is broader; it is for the family, the nucleus of which is the marital bond. Marriage is God's invention, and He intended this lifelong, exclusive union between a man and a woman to become the foundation upon which a family is built. I am convinced that a strong marriage will cover a multitude of difficulties in other areas, while a struggling marriage will undermine most hopes of building a healthy household. That's one reason I encourage young couples, ideally, to give their marriage time to solidify before having children.

When Cynthia and I began building our new home, we noticed that the general contractor poured the concrete slab, then waited a period of time before starting the framing. The soil in Texas is notoriously fickle, expanding and shrinking dramatically as moisture comes and goes. So he wanted to make sure the concrete had time to cure before adding the stress of equipment, stacks of building material, and the weight of walls and a roof.

As we discuss the characteristics of a healthy household, I want you to keep three issues in the front of your mind:

- how your original household has prepared you for marriage (the past),
- how you are consciously or unconsciously repeating the pattern established by that original model (the present), and
- what characteristics you want to define your marriage and family (the future).

CHARACTERISTICS OF A HEALTHY FAMILY

Back to the original question: what is a family? I decided to do what you would often do when you want to find the meaning of a word. I checked the dictionary and, admittedly, I was disappointed. Webster says, "A group of individuals living under one roof and usually under one head; a group of persons of common ancestry."[2] Not much help.

To be more thorough, I dusted off my giant, exhaustive *Oxford English Dictionary*, found the entry for *family*, pulled out my magnifying glass, and read, "The body of persons who live in one house or under one head, including parents, children, servants, etc."[3] OK, that was not *my* childhood home! As I recall, *I* was the servant! Maybe that fits Oxford, but it doesn't describe most of us. Here are my own thoughts as we begin to unravel this little mystery. See what you think.

The family is where we put down our first roots, where we form our most lasting impressions, where we put together the building blocks of our character, where we determine whether we will view life through the eyes of prejudice or acceptance. Family is where we learn to laugh and where we are allowed to weep without losing respect. Family is where we learn how to share, how to relate, how to treat other people. Family is where we learn how to interpret our surroundings correctly. It's where we discover, in practical terms, how to draw the line between right and wrong, between good and evil. Dysfunctional families blur that line, and boundaries become unclear. Solid, secure families have a clear view of the difference so that its members have very little ethical confusion. Moral dilemmas will challenge us, but people from healthy families are seldom unclear about what's right or wrong.

Rather than rely solely on my own opinions and my own perspective, I did some research among several experts.

Having studied the work of a number of respected sources, I put together a list of eight characteristics that describe a healthy family. This is a composite of characteristics that appear consistently on the lists of those who have spent half their lives working in the trenches with families—counselors, psychologists, psychiatrists, researchers, and authors. This is certainly not an exhaustive list, but it's the most significant traits of a healthy household common to the cross-section of experts I studied.

First, *the members of the household are committed to one another.* The family, therefore, is a unit with members dedicated to living their lives in support of one another with unquestioned loyalty.

Second, *they spend time together.* A wholesome, healthy family believes that time together cannot have quality without sufficient quantity.

Third, *they enjoy open, frequent communication.* No question is irrelevant or inappropriate, no opinion is disrespected, and no subject is considered off-limits. Important, life-determining subjects are quite naturally intermingled with the mundane.

Fourth, *the family turns inward during times of crisis.* Members of wholesome, healthy families work through difficulties together. A crisis brings them closer because

they look within the family for strength rather than looking to something outside.

Fifth, *the family members express affirmation and
encouragement often.* "Good job!" "You have such talent!"
"I admire you for that!" "You mean a lot to me!"

By the way, affirmation and encouragement are different. We affirm who people are, while we encourage what
people do. Both are important. Both are necessary to help
others discover who they are and what they do well, which
builds a strong sense of personal security. We aren't born
with a well-defined sense of self; we discover ourselves
through the influence of those important to us. And we're
never too old to discover more.

Sixth, *the family members share a spiritual commitment.*
Family is important, but not supreme. The family members are bound in unity by their shared relationship with
God, and they learn to nurture it as a result of mutual
encouragement.

Seventh, *each person in the household trusts the others
and values the trust he or she has earned.* This trust is built
upon mutual respect and a dedication to truth.

Eighth, *the members enjoy freedom and grace.* Each has
the freedom to try new things, think different thoughts,
embrace values and perspectives that may be new to the

family, even challenge old ways of doing things. And all of this is built upon grace. Everyone has the freedom to fail, the freedom to be completely wrong, the freedom to have faults and weaknesses without fear of rejection or condemnation. In a grace-based environment, failure is kept in perspective so that members of the family have enough confidence to recover and grow and achieve.

How does that sound? As you look back, how well did your original family prepare you to have a marriage with these eight characteristics? We're not looking to blame anyone, but we want to take a realistic inventory of the training we received in the art of marriage building. No family is perfect, so all of us can look back and find at least one characteristic that won't come naturally to us because we never saw it modeled, or we saw it modeled poorly.

Looking at your household now, what healthy and unhealthy characteristics have you brought along without realizing it? We all have some good we can build upon as well as some things we need to change. Do an honest appraisal of your marriage as it is today. Without being too hard on yourself, what responsibility can you take for those characteristics that are lacking in your marriage?

As we look to the future, I want to glean from the book of Ephesians some action points you can use to transform the environment of your household. I encourage you to keep your focus on your marriage. Because that's the nucleus of the home, whatever you do to restore its health and strength will naturally restore what's broken among the other relationships. If you have no children yet, this will make a comfortable nest for them to begin life well. If you have children, the changes you make in your marriage will affect the rest of the household more quickly and dramatically than you think. And if you plan to have no children, your marriage can be a warm, hospitable place for your extended family and friends to find refuge.

BUILDING YOUR MARRIAGE WITH NEW MATERIAL

In the last three chapters of Ephesians, I find at least a half dozen guidelines that will transform your marriage, giving your family what it needs to thrive. I have mentioned some before, so I will be brief. Others will require further explanation, mostly to dispel some false notions that have corrupted the message of this wonderful letter on unity.

Pursue Truth

> Therefore, laying aside falsehood, speak truth each one of you with his neighbor, for we are members of one another. (Ephesians 4:25)

This is a life principle that cannot be stressed enough. Relationships are built on trust, and trust is built on truth. The more you lie, withhold honesty, or hide behind a false image, the more you weaken the relationship. I am often amazed at how many couples lie to each other, how many relationships are built upon deception. In the process of counseling a couple, a fact or a viewpoint will come out of one partner to the complete and utter shock of the other. Mouths drop open and a look will flash from one to the other accompanied by the words, "I didn't know that!" Why didn't he or she know? To put it bluntly, because the spouse is lying or won't declare the whole truth. Both are lethal to the marriage.

Exercise Restraint and Courtesy

> Let no unwholesome word proceed from your mouth, but only such a word as is good for edification according to the need of the moment, so that it will give grace to those who hear. . . . Let all bitterness and wrath and anger and clamor and slander be put away from you, along with all malice. Be kind to one another, tender-hearted, forgiving each other, just as God in Christ also has forgiven you. (Ephesians 4:29, 31–32)

I have long said that love without truth is deceptive, and truth without love is cruel. Love and truth very naturally go together. Unfortunately, the tongue can quickly tear down what love so carefully builds. So let me highlight a few terms in these verses.

I explained in a previous chapter that the word translated "unwholesome" means rotten or putrid, which implies that certain speech has a contaminating effect on another. It's like slipping a rotten piece of meat into your mate's sandwich or cooking for him or her an omelet contaminated with salmonella. Why would you want to destroy the internal health of someone you love so much? Yet that's what criticism, insults, put-downs, sarcasm, bickering, and profanity do to your mate and others.

Speech like that usually arises from sour attitudes like bitterness, wrath, anger, clamor, and malice. The Greek term for "bitterness" originally meant sharp or pointed like an arrow. It has all the same connotations that we attach to it in English. "Let all sharpness be put away from you." It's a word that describes a spirit that refuses to be reconciled because of long-standing resentments. Each lingering offense is like a porcupine's quill—the more of those you have, the more injurious you become to others, even when you don't mean to be.

Wrath and anger go together, but they are not the

same. The word for "wrath" is probably better translated "fury," referring to outbursts of passionate rage, shouting, tantrums. Anger is a close cousin, but it lacks the impulsiveness of fury. This would be more of a sullen, hostile attitude that acts with greater awareness and deliberation.

Clamor is a word we don't use much these days. The Greek word means "to croak or cry with a loud and raucous voice."[4] Clamor includes insulting, sarcastic putdowns that are expressed brashly. When I see one partner take sarcastic jabs at the other in a public gathering, supposedly in good fun (at the other's expense), I see a marriage headed for trouble.

On the positive side, we see the words "kind," "tenderhearted," and "forgiving" in verse 32. In stating the principle, I used the word *courtesy*. Courtesy is something we usually extend to strangers, isn't it? We aren't courteous to the people most familiar to us because, allegedly, we're past that stage of the relationship. We can afford to be "real" with each other, we often hear. Unfortunately, many want to see "real" and "rude" as synonymous when it comes to their life partners. The next time your partner does something to irritate you and a volley of harsh words loads into the firing chamber of your mind, stop and mentally unload as you ask yourself, "How would I respond to a guest in my home if he or she were to do what my mate is doing now?" That's the courtesy we should be extending to one another on a daily basis.

Learn to Cooperate and Adapt

> Be subject to one another in the fear of Christ.
> (Ephesians 5:21)

This verse, originally written to members of a church, comes on the heels of several commands. "Be filled with the Spirit" (v. 18), "speak to one another in psalms and hymns" (v. 19), "giving thanks for all things" (v. 20). Then this command appears. And don't overlook the motivation: "in the fear of Christ." "Fear," in this sense, means to be motivated by a reverential respect.

Submission is a tough word to use in today's culture because the idea of subservience is unthinkable. However, Jesus Christ, the supreme Creator of space, time, earth and everything in it didn't have a problem with being subservient, and He calls us to do the same. But—I repeat—we don't want to be subservient to anyone, least of all those who owe every effort to making us happy. (The effects of the Fall are alive and well in marriages.) Nevertheless, submission has everything to do with love and nothing to do with a pecking order in the kingdom, in the church, and especially in the home.

Submission is the willingness to cooperate with and adapt to the needs and the desires of those we love. Note that the submission is mutual: "Be subject to one another." That submission takes different forms, depending upon the situation and the relationship; so there are no hard-and-fast rules for submission—only a spirit that cooperates and adapts itself to the needs of the situation and the person involved.

In verse 22, wives are encouraged to make this cooperating and adapting to their husbands a regular part of their relationship with God. Unfortunately, the culture of Ephesus and much of the surrounding world viewed women as objects to be used, little more than commodities to be owned. Treasured by some, to be sure, but owned nonetheless. Women in that day had little other choice but to "be subject." So Paul's desire was to raise the issue of submission for women from mere legal subjugation to give it the dignity of Christlikeness that it deserves.

Paul apparently wanted to tread so lightly on the issue that he left the verb out of the sentence, borrowing the concept from the previous sentence. The Greek reads, literally, "Wives, to your own husbands, as to the Lord." Because the concept of submission is so thoroughly Christian, he saw no need to change it for women, choosing instead to give the idea its proper focus. The story was quite different for men, however. Remember that the concept of submission is mutual. Both husbands and wives are commanded to be cooperative and adaptable to each other. (If you're a husband, read that *again*!) However, women may struggle with one aspect of this accommodation, while men wrestle with another. And this introduces the next action point.

Demonstrate Christlike Love

Husbands, love your wives, just as Christ also loved the church and gave Himself up for her. (Ephesians 5:25)

Now, *this* was, to the people of that culture, something completely revolutionary. The historical evidence shows that men of that time and place, just as now and here, loved their wives with deep conviction and genuine emotion. The caricature of the brash, uncaring ogre treating his wife like livestock has no basis in history. However, the love was more typically the passionate, self-gratifying *eros*, or perhaps at times, the loyal and noble *philos*. However, guess which word Paul chose.

You're right! He chose *agape*, the kind of love Christ demonstrates and demands. Christlike love is by nature submissive. In the male-centered culture of the Greeks and Romans, the command for a man to love a woman as he would his own flesh elevated the value of women to that of equal, if not superior! Let's face it, women often struggle with self-loathing, but we men typically suffer from the opposite affliction. There are certainly exceptions, but few men fail to love themselves enough. For men, loving someone sacrificially—as Christ loved His church—is submission.

Allow me to be bold with an observation and to be as clear as I can on what I believe to be the scriptural view of men and women in marriage. Leadership in the home rests with the husband, making this issue of selfless love primary. If men take the lead in demonstrating Christlike love—the duty we are so quick to neglect—all of the areas of life we feel so compelled to dominate would delight to rest in our leadership. I have rarely seen a woman who was loved "as Christ loved the church" who had any difficulty adapting and cooperating with her husband. When there's a problem in that area, more often than not, I have found that the issue was the husband's—not always, but usually. That kind of love inspires adaptation and cooperation in others.

These two principles, by the way, are two sides of the same coin, and they are not exclusive to either gender. As followers of Jesus Christ, we should be characterized by mutual submission and selfless love, just like He was. Paul said these would encourage unity in the church. Pause long enough to imagine how they could transform your marriage.

Show Respect for Authority

> Children, obey your parents in the Lord, for this is right. (Ephesians 6:1)

How long is someone a child? Certainly anyone living under the roof of his or her parents qualifies, and so he or she should offer due respect. But what happens when the man or woman "leaves" the original family in order to be joined to a mate and establish a new family? I said earlier that the Greek term for "leave" is most often translated "abandon." How does the parent-child relationship then change? What remains?

Paul had no fewer than six Greek terms to choose from, and he chose a noun that is derived from the verb "to bear." This applies to anyone who was born of someone else. Pull up your shirt, glance just above your beltline, and if you see a navel, this includes you. The command means, literally, "hearken to, give ear to, attend to."

To the son or daughter still living under a parent's roof, this has a literal, direct application: *do what you're told.*

Once married, the relationship changes; however, the respect does not. The parent releases the child to be joined to a partner and be subject to him or her, and no longer has authority in the former sense. Instead, the parent becomes a mentor, a source of wisdom, a guide. Unfortunately, I see too many young married men and women throw this command to respect their parents to the wind and, instead, show incredible disrespect to their mom and dad. This is not only insolent, it's downright stupid. Furthermore, it says a great deal about how they regard authority in general.

I love it when a young couple marries, and each partner takes an active role in building up the relationship between his or her spouse and in-laws. The couple stands together, depending upon each other, looking within the marriage for emotional support and enrichment, yet both remain open to receiving the advice of their parents. They are adults, so they make their own decisions, but they don't regard parental wisdom as an intrusion. They receive it graciously and heed wise counsel where appropriate.

Showing respect for parents will help create a peaceful marriage. When one or both partners struggle with authority issues, strife between them is inevitable. Respect for parents translates into respect for the boss, respect for the law, respect for church leadership, and ultimately respect for the Lord. And because each married partner has a certain amount of authority over the other, authority issues will soon divide them.

Stand Strong Against the Real Enemy

> Finally, be strong in the Lord and in the strength of His might. Put on the full armor of God, so that you will be able to stand firm against the schemes of the devil. (Ephesians 6:10–11)

Marital difficulties can come in a number of different disguises, but you can know for sure that behind all of them is a very active and aggressive adversary who wants to see you fail. He slips into your home uninvited, looks for an opportunity, then takes full advantage of any weakness he can find.

A number of years ago, a church member told me about a chilling encounter she had on an airplane. When the meal was served, she noticed that the man sitting next to her didn't eat his. While everyone else ate, he periodically bowed his head and closed his eyes, apparently in prayer. As the flight attendants gathered the empty trays, he handed his back untouched.

My friend said, "I noticed you were praying. Are you a Christian?"

He replied, "No, actually, I am a satanist. Our coven hopes to see one hundred Christian leaders fail in their marriages this year. We are fasting and praying to Satan with that in mind."

That is the true enemy. You may think your only problems are a tragic past, financial difficulties, excessive emotional baggage, meddling in-laws, rebellious children, poor communication, an unsubmissive partner, and all the rest. All of those challenges are significant on their own, and I don't mean to suggest that Satan is behind every difficulty. However, he will take advantage of any opportunity you leave to him. He will even make use of your best intentions and good deeds. As one insightful author writes,

Satan doesn't come to the Christian and tempt him to transparent evil. To presume Satan will attack us at our strong point defies good sense. No, instead he will tempt us at the weakest point of our defenses where we have forgotten his capabilities. He will not mount a direct attack on our strengths. He will look for our vulnerabilities, the places where we do not think defenses are needed.

For example, Satan will not tempt you to hate your family; he will tempt you to absentmindedly let your good deeds consume your time until you are out serving Christ five nights a week. The result for your family will be the same as if you hated them. Mission accomplished![5]

So, how do you combat this threat? In two ways: prevailing prayer and persistent awareness.

With all prayer and petition pray at all times in the Spirit, and with this in view, be on the alert with all perseverance and petition for all the saints. (Ephesians 6:18)

Satan is powerful, but he's not omnipotent, omniscient, or omnipresent. He's mostly limited to the opportunities you leave him. And always remember: his chief weapon is deception. Prayer is your first defense. Pray for a clear vision of what's going on in your family, what difficulties your spouse is facing, what changes your children are enduring. Then pray for each member specifically and by name. Bring the things they're going through before the Lord. And in the place of fretting or worrying, pray.

Second, remain vigilant or "alert with all perseverance." Pay attention, watch for signs, listen sensitively, look when nothing is being said, concentrate your full attention on those you love. Pay attention to attitudes, discover where your mate's struggles are. Use your observation to keep the lines of communication open with your mate. Be the refuge where your mate can retreat and unload all the cares and concerns without your feeling the need to advise or fix. Then commit to praying as a couple.

Handling difficulties promptly is your best defense against your adversary. Don't allow them to go unattended.

As you review the memories of your original family and take an honest look at the marriage you are building now, what do you see? Chances are good that you are repeating some patterns you found unpleasant. Strange isn't it? Yet, very common. Fortunately you have a new pattern to follow. Straight from the pages of Scripture is a list of family values guaranteed to turn your marriage into the opening exhibit of a wonderful museum of memories.

Seven

Danger Signs of Marital Erosion

The citizens of a small township just north of Pittsburgh took great care in the design and construction of a brand new, red-brick building that would house the police department and a few other city offices. The architecture and engineering were sound, the craftsmanship superb, and everybody's spirits were high at the ribbon cutting as the townspeople celebrated the opening of their fine building.

A couple of months passed and someone in the front office noticed that opening her window took a little more effort than it used to. Soon it wouldn't close completely. Talk around the water cooler confirmed that she wasn't the only one. Others had experienced problems with doors dragging and cracks forming here and there. Before long, a noticeable crack on the outside brickwork ran along the mortar and up two stories. A little later, a few bricks began to fall as it became clear that the whole structure was breaking apart. Eventually, officials had to condemn the building that had been the pride of the community.

An investigation confirmed what had been happening in other structures around the area. A number of historic buildings were beginning to collapse after standing strong for a hundred years and more. The culprit proved to be a controversial coal-mining process called longwall mining, deep in the earth beneath the foundation. Multiple tons of subsurface soil, rock, and coal had been removed, leaving the new building resting on a foundation that had no reliable support. Because of this man-made erosion, the building was literally sinking.

Erosion always takes a serious toll. Since it works silently, slowly, subtly, and ever so steadily, it poses an insidious danger as it destroys what people carefully build.

What happens to a building can happen in a life. We start out by receiving Christ's free gift of salvation, acknowledging that He bore the penalty of our sin, and trusting Him alone for eternal life. We submit to His leadership and His authority over our lives and begin to build our lives around His principles. However, in the process of time, cracks begin to form because of character flaws and poor choices, unsuspected and unnoticed by others and ignored by us. A compromise here, a slip there, a little tolerated contamination in one area of life followed by yet another. And before long, the whole structure stands on the verge of complete collapse. Erosion.

The same kind of process that breaks a building apart or destroys a Christian's life can reduce a marriage to rubble along with the family that's built around it. After more than four decades of administering vows to beaming, hopeful couples, I've seen it happen more times than I care to count. Each marriage begins strong with two people committed to Jesus Christ. They recite meaningful vows before the Lord and a gathering of witnesses. They start their lives together with Him at the center of their marriage. They enjoy a harmony and romance of which they'd once only dreamed. Everything is good . . . they would say *great*.

After the honeymoon, reality returns as life kicks in. So does the process of erosion—busyness, demands, deadlines, bills, pressure, spats, and disappointments. Then along come children and their relentless needs, their many activities, and their all-consuming demand on our time and attention. I sometimes laugh to myself when I hear a couple experiencing marital difficulty saying they've decided that maybe having a child will help. Believe me, I don't laugh because it's funny.

None of this is new. I find these same issues afflicting the lives of ancient people as I read the pages of an ancient book. In the book of 1 Samuel, we find the story of a godly man, a faithful servant of God rearing two sons of natural offspring and one by adoption. There's no mention of a wife, so bear with me. The life we will examine has relevance to marriage even though the plot of this story doesn't revolve around a marriage.

A Domestic Erosion Observed

This example of domestic erosion can be found in 1 Samuel 1–4. Allow me to introduce you to the members of the family, starting with the father.

Eli

Eli was both high priest and judge, busy about his work, directing the affairs of the temple and leading the nation of Israel. In those days, God raised up a person to fulfill the duties of a king, only without all the trappings of royalty. Eli served in both of these roles for forty years, and his work consumed much of his attention. With the rituals of the temple, political affairs, wars, treaties, civic projects, demands, and decisions to make, his boys, Hophni and Phinehas, were left to rear themselves.

We know from details given later in the story that Eli was advanced in years and extremely overweight. Nevertheless, he was a good priest, an able leader, spiritually sensitive, and devoted to God. This was a venerable, seasoned servant of the Lord who had earned the respect of his people, the Jewish nation. However, Scripture tells us that by the end of his life, "his eyes were set so that he could not see" (4:15). This is a twist of literary irony, obliquely intended to comment on his family life. He had lost touch with his sons and turned a blind eye to what they had become. Let's meet them next.

Hophni and Phinehas

Hophni and Phinehas had become priests like their father; however, they could not have been more opposed to everything he taught and lived. According to Scripture, "The sons of Eli were worthless men; they did not know the LORD and the custom of the priests with the people" (2:12–13). They were not the last preacher or priest to serve in the ministry without knowing the Lord. That reality continues to this present day.

Let me pause to caution you. Pay close attention to the life of the one you choose to follow as a spiritual leader. Be very discerning when you listen to a teacher on the radio or watch him or her on television. Be careful to observe and evaluate what is said and what is not said. Read with a critical eye what they write and always check it against Scripture. Watch how they lead and examine how they live. Here were boys who donned the official robes of a priest and stood in sacred places where a priest stands, accepting the respect of an unwary public. Yet a mere glance into their private lives would have revealed the ugly truth.

Verse 12 of chapter 2 leaves no room for doubt that the young men were "worthless." They had no plans to repent. They were well established in their ways, too set, too stubborn and rebellious to change. In fact, when their father confronted them, Scripture says, "They would not listen to the voice of their father" (2:25).

Samuel

In contrast to Eli's worthless natural sons, we have Eli's adopted son, Samuel. He was born to a woman named Hannah, who promised the Lord that if He would give her a son in spite of her infertility, she would give him back once he was weaned. And true to her word, she brought young Samuel to grow up and serve in the tabernacle. Eli reared the boy and mentored him in the ways of the priesthood.

Here we have three boys reared by the same man, in identical settings, by the same rules, but what a difference. Samuel reminds me of a beautiful rose growing in soil above a cesspool. In this vile, corrupt environment, he somehow avoids the contamination of his adopted brothers and grows to love the Lord. Perhaps Eli realized that his sons were beyond help and tried to do better by Samuel. Who knows?

The Crisis

We cannot know for sure how the problem started or how long it took for Hophni and Phinehas to become so depraved, but it had to have been brewing for a long time. As F. B. Meyer noted, "No man suddenly becomes base." Among their sins were these offenses: they used their positions for personal gain (2:29), stole meat intended for sacrifice (2:15–16), threatened worshipers with violence (2:16), despised their father (2:25), and even had sex with the women who came to serve in the tabernacle (2:22). No wonder the Lord calls them "worthless"! They were vile, cynical, rebellious, and lustful. Their consciences had become so calloused that they didn't even bother to hide their sins, which became a public scandal.

During all of this, Eli had been warned several times. Offended and irate worshipers had informed him repeatedly. Note Eli's rebuke:

> He said to them, "Why do you do such things, the evil things that *I hear from all these people*? No, my sons; for

the report is not good which *I hear the* LORD'*s people circulating*." (1 Samuel 2:23–24; emphasis added)

Suddenly, an unnamed prophet appeared to Eli and delivered these words from the Lord:

Why do you kick at My sacrifice and at My offering which I have commanded in My dwelling, and honor your sons above Me, by making yourselves fat with the choicest of every offering of My people Israel? (1 Samuel 2:29)

The prophet followed this with a pronouncement of judgment on Eli and his sons. If they did not repent, all three would soon be dead. We see from this that the Lord held Eli accountable for the actions of his sons. While turning a blind eye, he conveniently failed to ask why his dinner table was so full. No doubt, that was the cause of his obesity.

He also received a warning from the young boy in his charge. You may remember the story of how Samuel heard God's voice in the night. At first he thought Eli was calling to him, so he ran to where the old priest was sleeping to see what he wanted. But each time, Eli sent the boy back to his bed, perhaps thinking the voice was a dream.

By the third time, Eli discerned that the voice belonged to God and instructed Samuel on how to respond.

> And Eli said to Samuel, "Go lie down, and it shall be if He calls you, that you shall say, 'Speak, LORD, for Your servant is listening.' " So Samuel went and lay down in his place. Then the LORD came and stood and called as at other times, "Samuel! Samuel!" And Samuel said, "Speak, for Your servant is listening." (1 Samuel 3:9–10)

As a child in Sunday school, I remember seeing pictures of young Samuel and hearing this fascinating story of God speaking to the little boy. I, like every other child, could see myself in the story, and I remember wishing it would happen to me. I always wondered what it was that the Lord said, but the story always ended there. Now I understand why my teachers left the rest of the story out. Samuel's first message from God was a chilling pronouncement of judgment on Eli and his sons.

> The LORD said to Samuel, "Behold, I am about to do a thing in Israel at which both ears of everyone who hears it will tingle. In that day I will carry out against Eli all that I have spoken concerning his house, from

beginning to end. For I have told him that I am about to judge his house forever for the iniquity which he knew, because his sons brought a curse on themselves and he did not rebuke them. Therefore I have sworn to the house of Eli that the iniquity of Eli's house shall not be atoned for by sacrifice or offering forever." (1 Samuel 3:11–14)

Eli had been warned many times over many years. His sons sinned in the tabernacle. When the people told him, he gave his sons little more than a scolding and a slap on the wrist, which is tantamount to giving them permission to continue.

Indeed, the sin did continue and worsen, so the Lord sent a prophet to pronounce judgment as a warning. In the written account of that episode, a clue suggests that Eli had moved from being merely a passive bystander to an active participant. Eli didn't personally steal meat from the worshipers, but his expanding girth suggested that he savored every stolen morsel at the dinner table.

Why do you kick at My sacrifice and at My offering which I have commanded in My dwelling, and honor your sons above Me, *by making yourselves fat* with the choicest of every offering of My people Israel? (1 Samuel 2:29; emphasis added)

This crisis began with a tiny crack, a small infraction of the rules, then slowly enlarged over time to where it became a public offense. The rampant, shameless sin of the priests compromised the integrity of the tabernacle, cast a shadow over the covenant, and worst of all, called into question the character of God. Erosion. Silent, slow, subtle, steady erosion.

The Response

The fact that sin was present in Eli's household is no surprise, and he is no more deserving of condemnation for that than any of us. Sin is universal. Difficulties will come upon every family. The dangers of erosion threaten the stability of every marriage. The problem lay in his response—or, rather, his complete lack of such. Take note of how Eli reacted to the message through Samuel.

So Samuel lay down until morning. Then he opened the doors of the house of the LORD. But Samuel was afraid to tell the vision to Eli. Then Eli called Samuel and said, "Samuel, my son." And he said, "Here I am." He said, "What is the word that He spoke to you? Please do not hide it from me. May God do so to you, and more also, if you hide anything from me of all the words that He spoke to you." So Samuel told him everything and hid nothing from him. And he said, "It is the LORD; let Him do what seems good to Him." (1 Samuel 3:15–18)

How would you respond if a messenger from the Lord stepped into your world and told you that He was going to destroy your household and remove your family? Whatever your reaction, I suspect it would be more than, "Oh well. So be it." Eli's is a classic response of a passive father. He just couldn't be bothered with such concerns when it came to his own home. He led the tabernacle as high priest. He led the nation as judge. But somehow he expected the tough decisions concerning his sons to work themselves out.

THE DANGER SIGNS OF MARITAL EROSION

What signs indicate that a marriage is eroding? Probably not what you would think. All relationships have small cracks, creaking doors, and sticky windows from time to time. These are not nearly as important as how we respond to them.

The danger signs appear in how we take action when those subtle problems begin to occur, and they certainly will. Eli demonstrated a reckless apathy toward the sins of Hophni and Phinehas when their sins were minor. As their sins grew more blatant, pervasive, and scandalous, he felt increasingly powerless to address them. And by the time his boys were fully grown men, the only righteous, just answer to their completely depraved way of life was unthinkable—public exposure and, if they didn't repent, public stoning. In those days, God dealt severely with immoral and unethical priests.

MARITAL EROSION

Here are four danger signs that suggest marital erosion.

Too Busy

When you have only enough time and energy to handle the big things in life, the small but equally important ones go unattended. As Israel's high priest and judge, Eli had to have been very busy . . . too busy. Alexander Whyte, Scottish pastor of yesteryear, in his fine book *Bible Characters* writes,

> Away back, at the beginning of his life, Eli had taken far too much in hand. Eli was not a great man like

Moses or Aaron, but he took both the office of Moses and the office of Aaron upon his single self. Eli was both chief judge and the high priest in himself for the whole house of Israel. The ablest, the most laborious, the most devoted, the most tireless and sleepless of men could not have done what Eli undertook to do. . . .

And, taking up what was beyond mortal power to perform, the certain result was the he did nothing well.[1]

How busy are you? How are you doing with *quantity* time? Do you and your spouse have enough time together to enjoy easy and relaxing conversation, or do you spend most of it dealing with problems or addressing only practical matters? Do you regularly schedule time to be a couple? Looking at your schedule and your to-do list, what has first priority? When family and work vie for the same time slot, which most often wins? When you arrive at the end of your life, which would you rather have people say of you, "She was a good wife to her husband/He was a good husband to his wife" or "Now there goes a dedicated professional"?

See any cracks? Of course, you do. Nearly everyone does. The real question is, how will you respond?

Too Dull

Dull is not a kind word, but it's appropriate. Eli remained insensitive to the words of caution he received from the people and from the prophet. For whatever reason, he didn't react with the kind of urgency we would expect. He failed to connect any of the dots . . . even the obvious ones. The gravity of the warnings didn't have the emotional impact they should have had. Amazingly, the prediction that he and his sons would die evoked little more than a shrug.

How sensitive are you to subtle signals? How aware are you of your mate's unhappiness? Are you too distracted or self-absorbed to notice those tiny cracks in your relationship? Have you heard understated comments that grabbed your attention or piqued your curiosity? If so, how did you respond? Did you blow it off, or did you pause to probe deeper? Have you noticed that your mate is too quiet or often sad, overly stressed, or preoccupied? Have you taken time to discover what he or she may be feeling or enduring?

Have you noticed any subtle problems? Who hasn't? The key question is, what will you do?

Too Slow

Eli failed to move quickly in response to the warnings of people who genuinely cared. He waited until his sons were men before he intervened and, by then, they were hardened in their rebellion and calloused by cynicism.

Responding promptly to issues as they arise can keep most marital issues manageable. So, may I ask? How long do you wait before you discuss edgy matters with your mate? Do you address hurts and sources of anger right away, or do you put them off for a more convenient time? What about counseling? Does an issue have to reach critical mass before you'll make an appointment with someone who is qualified to offer biblical, practical guidance?

Allow me to probe deeper. Do you know of any lingering issues that need to be resolved? Any past conflict that didn't find closure? Do you find yourself waiting to deal with acute issues because you're not sure how to approach them? Why wait? What is gained by procrastinating? Procrastination feeds erosion.

Too Easy

When Eli did act, the intensity of his response didn't match the gravity of the difficulty. Let's revisit the conversation.

Now Eli was very old; and he heard all that his sons were doing to all Israel, and how they lay with the women who served at the doorway of the tent of meeting. He said to them, "Why do you do such things, the evil things that I hear from all these people? No, my sons; for the report is not good which I hear the LORD's people circulating. If one man sins against another, God will mediate for him; but if a man sins against the LORD, who can intercede for him?" (1 Samuel 2:22–25)

These are fine words. This is the very rebuke his boys needed to hear . . . *years* earlier! To put this into perspective, as I mentioned before, the sins of Hophni and Phinehas were punishable by death. Even if he couldn't bring himself to execute his own sons, certainly the situation warranted expulsion from the temple at the very least.

Perhaps he knew what needed to be done and put it off, or maybe he had bigger fires to fight in the early days. When the sins finally became a priority, the drastic action they demanded was more than he could bring himself to do. And don't forget, Eli's own participation in their sin dulled the edge of his taking action. His pathetic, inadequate response accomplished nothing except to dishonor the Lord.

We cannot afford to allow our love to override our judgment. Most situations require tenderness; however, some demand toughness. By "tough," I don't mean harsh or abusive. Toughness is the willingness to do what is personally hard to do. When we are willing to do what is right despite the great personal cost, our priorities are revealed. That's why the Lord confronted Eli with these strong words: "You honor your sons above Me."

What if the difficulty you discover requires a significant change? Are you willing to change jobs, or live somewhere less tempting, or downsize your lifestyle to give your marriage the attention it deserves? Can you make significant adjustments to your life and routine without resenting your mate for it? If you know something is eroding your marriage, and you are unwilling to act decisively, even sacrificially, what does that say about your priorities?

What are you willing to sacrifice for the health of your marriage? What are you willing to do for the highest, greatest good of your mate? Tough questions like these, answered honestly, reveal how serious you are to step up and stop the erosion.

How to Respond

I have asked a lot of questions. Most of them imply their own answers, but I don't want to stop there. I want to offer three two-word responses to trouble that will help avoid the need for drastic action. Each time you see a subtle problem, think of these three responses in this order— one, two, three—and carry them out immediately. I promise they will make a difference.

Wake Up!

Intelligent, thoughtful, diligent people can be blind to needs at home. Home is supposed to be a refuge from a demanding world populated with demanding people. Consequently, it's easy to relax so much that we become dull to the needs of our closest companion. Decide today to be more aware.

Then, wide awake, when you see something that grabs your attention, don't ignore it. Don't shrug it off, assuming that it's nothing. It might be, but don't merely dismiss it. Trust your instincts enough to take your observation seriously. Then . . .

Talk Straight!

Lay aside accusations and defensiveness as you commit yourself to communicating. Speak plainly and clearly about what you have observed without attacking or accusing. Gently present your perspective. In place of accusations, ask questions. Then listen. Seek to understand your partner's point of view. Keep at it until you have a similar perspective of the situation. Maintain a constant check on your motives as you communicate. Talk to understand and to be understood. Any speech that doesn't accomplish this goal is futile. When you arrive at a common understanding of the situation . . .

Stay Close!

Work with your partner to handle any difficulty as a team. Decide, together, how each of you will adjust in response to the problem. Because you are not a parent to your mate, you can suggest adjustments that might be helpful, but only your partner can make his or her decision. Your role is to stay close, remain committed, and be your spouse's ally, confidant, sounding board, and mirror as the Holy Spirit does His work on the inside. Commit to knowing your mate intimately, which means you must never assume you know all there is to know. This perspective will help make your marriage a lifelong journey of mutual discovery.

Keep First Things First

Addressing marital erosion need not be complicated. It requires only two essentials: listening to your life partner and giving your marriage first priority. It may surprise you to know that John Wesley, founder of the Methodist movement, did neither. Wesley's tireless work as a preacher and spiritual leader brought many thousands of people to a saving knowledge of Jesus Christ. All who study his life and learn of his accomplishments cannot help being impressed. However, his marriage to Molly Goldhawk Vazeille was a miserable failure. In this respect, he reminds me of Eli.

Some say Molly's jealousy and violent temper destroyed the marriage but that notwithstanding, Wesley was not merely passive as a husband, the man was downright neglectful. According to him, "no Methodist preacher should 'preach one sermon or travel one day less in a married than in a single state.'"[2]

After three botched courtships as a younger man, the forty-seven-year-old bachelor minister was introduced to Molly, a widow close to his own age. After courting for just a little more than two weeks, they were married, though few understood why. Her nominal, conventional spirituality seemed a very odd match to his profoundly deep commitment to the Lord.

The first sign of trouble came just after the wedding. In explaining to his fellow Methodists why he had married so quickly, he said that his marriage was "a cross that he had taken up" in order to "break down the prejudice about the world and him." Within the week, he was at a conference and then off for one of his long preaching tours. He justified his actions with the words, "In respect of traveling abroad, the Methodist preacher who has a wife should be as though he had none." Understandably, these two events broke Molly's heart.

Wesley continued his extensive traveling and preaching. And he continued his intimate counseling of women, despite Molly's pleading that he stop. It's extremely doubtful that he ever did anything inappropriate, but the privacy that he kept and the adoring response he often received from other women didn't look appropriate. Molly begged him to stop his correspondence and private meetings with one particular young woman who had been converted after having married three men with not a single divorce on record. Her complaints were met with browbeating and the self-righteous claim that all of his actions were "for the cause of God."

Molly tried joining him on his preaching tours, but he refused to alter his habit of pressing on despite rain, cold, and bad roads. She tried remaining home, only to suffer the accusation that she didn't support her husband as she ought. She appealed to his brother, Charles, and other Methodist brethren to intercede, but they largely sided with John, labeling her with all sorts of unflattering epithets.

One biographer characterized the twenty-plus year

marriage as "largely nominal and often almost irrelevant; separation frequent, but never final until 1776; perennial mutual resentment."[3] On one of the many occasions when Molly left him, Wesley wrote in his journal, "For what cause I know not, my wife set out for Newcastle, purposing never to return. *Non eam reliqui; non dimisi; non revocabo.*" ('I have not left her; I have not sent her away; I shall not ask her to come back.')[4]

By the time he died at age eighty-seven, he had ridden over 250,000 miles (mainly on horseback), crossed the Irish sea forty-two times, and preached 40,000 sermons. The pace and the nature of his ministry never slowed, duty to his mate notwithstanding. She left him the final time in 1776, and they lived apart until she died five years later. Wesley was in London when he heard that his wife had died two days before.

Commenting on marriage and ministry, Wesley often said that if Mrs. Wesley had been a better wife and conducted herself as she should have, he might have been unfaithful to the great work that God had chosen for him. Strange thinking. Obviously, Wesley was married to his work first and regarded Molly as a distraction rather than his devoted partner in life and ministry.

My purpose in telling this story is not to denigrate John Wesley, but to illustrate that even the most "spiritually mature person" can allow his or her marriage to fail. All that's required are misplaced priorities and ignoring the danger signs.

Marital erosion didn't stop with a priest named Eli or with a preacher named Wesley. It's going on today in the community where you reside, in the place where you work, in the church where you worship. Marital erosion is a reality you cannot change . . . except in the home where you live.

The question is, will you?

Eight

Staying Young As Your Family Grows Older

Naught cared this body for wind or weather
When Youth and I lived in 't together.
—SAMUEL TAYLOR COLERIDGE

There's something delightful and carefree about youth. And when you share it with your mate, that season of springtime love can be doubly fun. Remember those days? The winsome, carefree evenings full of laughter, the gratifying romance and lovemaking, the resilience in the face of difficulties, the complete lack of fear, the excitement of having your whole future in front of you? All of that prompts a major question: why must that attitude stop? Who wrote the law that says that all gray or white hair should be dyed brown or black? What medical journal classified age as a disease? And who says that marriage has to lose its youthful zest, joy, and vitality?

171

Oh, I know. I'm not living in denial. The body won't last forever. As Erma Bombeck once said, "It's a quick slide from bikinis to estrogen." For men, hair stops growing where it should and starts growing like crazy where hair has no business growing! Gravity and age will eventually have its way with all of us. And like bangs, bruises, injuries, sickness, and accidents can wear down the body, the relentless challenges of everyday life can age a marriage—perhaps beyond its years. But is that really necessary? Is it inevitable? I say absolutely not! Why should married life lose its youthful enjoyment if we're still healthy and active, and leaning forward into life instead of casting a longing look over our shoulders at what used to be?

What I'm talking about is a perspective, an attitude, a frame of mind that sees life not as something to be endured or survived, but *lived*! One of my favorite baseball players, Satchel Paige, called it "mind over matter." His family could only estimate that he was born on July 7, 1906, which became his official birthday for the record keepers. After dazzling crowds in the old Negro Leagues for twenty-two years, he pitched his first Major League baseball game for the Cleveland Indians in 1948 and faced the best hitters in the game (most of them half his age). In 1965, Paige pitched his last game; three shutout innings for the Kansas City A's . . . *at age sixty*!

Satchel rarely answered questions about his age, but on occasion, he would give a reporter his standard reply: "Age is a question of mind over matter. If you don't mind, it don't matter."

Henry David Thoreau put it well: "None are so old as those who have outlived enthusiasm." Satchel Paige never lost his enthusiasm for the game of baseball . . . or life, for that matter. Age eventually caught up with him as it will for all of us. But Paige's talent and his attitude kept him playing long after his age told him to hang up his spikes.

The same is true of your age and your approach to marriage. You may be standing at the very threshold of a long future with your mate. Or you may be a few miles down the road with a few additions to the family. You might even be like Cynthia and me—married over five decades with an undetermined number of years yet to be enjoyed. Wherever you are in life, let me assure you that this chapter is for you. This is not as much about age as it is about attitude—our chosen posture when presented with difficulties and that quality that gives marriage its youthful spark. Satchel Paige was enthusiastic as a sixty-year-old pitcher because he was enthusiastic at age nineteen when he hurled his first professional fastball. The same is true of marriage.

These chapters have taken us through several principles and applications. We learned about marriage as God had originally intended it and the effects of sin on that once-pure intimacy. We discovered the centrality of the Lord and His Word in keeping a marriage on target. We were reminded of the crucial role that commitment and selfless love play keeping the bond secure. And we underscored a number of strategies that will help us face the real challenges that all couples encounter.

Books on marriage can be dangerous in the wrong hands. Very often one partner shops the marriage section of the bookstore to find just the right tool in order to "fix" his or her mate. Hopefully, you found the chapters in this book impossible to put off on your partner. This chapter will be no exception. No one can choose your attitude. Only you can do that. This chapter is about your choice of attitude and how it will affect your marriage.

TAKING ON MARRIAGE WITH A GREAT ATTITUDE

The cares and challenges of life can beat you down, leaving little energy to invest in a marriage, to say nothing of enjoying it. You might be thinking that once better days come, you can do that. Unfortunately, you'll be waiting a long time before those "better days" arrive. The years you could have enjoyed are gone. Don't age before you're old. Keeping a youthful attitude will keep your marriage fun and exciting—at any age. And I really mean *any*.

In a moment, we'll examine the life of an Old
Testament hero whose attitude as a young man foreshad-
owed his boldness as an old man. But before we do, I want
to point out a few attitudes that I find common to those
outliving their enthusiasm. These sprout bitter buds in
youth, bloom wildly in the middle years, and bear their
poison fruit in old age. And they will sap your marriage of
joy along the way. I encourage you to examine yourself for
these thoughts and feelings when facing difficulty.

NEGATIVE ATTITUDES IN
THE FACE OF DIFFICULTY

The first negative attitude that can accompany aging is *a
sense of uselessness.* "I'm no good to anybody. I'm just in
everybody's way. Why am I still around?" Johann Goethe,
the German poet, wrote, "A useless life is early death."[1] It's
natural to feel useless when life has its knee on your chest
and difficult circumstances simply won't let you off your
back. But don't let this attitude cling to you. You'll die
before you die. And what's worse, you'll drag your partner
down with you.

The second attitude is *self-pity.* "Nobody cares about me
any more. Why should I bother to stay alive? Why should I
bother reaching out to anyone? If anyone really cared, they'd
come to me." Self-pity invariably leads to blame. Blame

leads to bitterness, and bitterness causes others to withdraw. Can you blame them? Self-pity is the first step to a kind of paradoxical game of pull me-push you. You want people to draw you close, but your bitterness pushes them away. Self-pity is most definitely an intimacy killer!

The third negative attitude is *fear*. "I need to be very careful. I need to avoid all dangers and all risks." Fear is a normal emotion that God gave us to help us sense and avoid danger. But we can be overwhelmed by it during stressful times. The world feels more and more danger-ous—especially when growing older—which can lead to a suspicious outlook, which quickly erodes to paranoia. Before long you'll even begin to see your spouse as a threat.

Of course as one wag put it, "Just because you're not paranoid doesn't mean they're not out to get you." The world is a dangerous place—full of disease, crime, natural disasters—all sorts of evil. But fear is a thief that steals our joy and robs us of peace. Fear makes all of those dangers real before we ever have to face them. In fact, we may never face most of those dangers, but if we're afraid, we'll draw the blinds and lock the doors in an attempt to shut out every peril. And in the process, we give up the very things we're afraid the world will take away.

Last, and perhaps the most devastating of these four negative attitudes, is that of *inappropriate remorse*. This is a mixture of guilt and regret for poor choices, or as Merriam-Webster puts it, "a gnawing distress arising from a sense of guilt for past wrongs: self-reproach."[2] This attitude is forever looking back over its shoulder with a deep, heavy sigh, thinking, *If only I hadn't . . . if only I had . . .* (You finish the sentence if those are your words.)

Almost everyone has regrets. Most look wistfully at what might have been had they not made such stupid mistakes here and there. Most older people can identify with the little poem "Sometimes" by Thomas S. Jones Jr.

> Across the fields of yesterday
> He sometimes comes to me,
> a little lad just back from play—
> The lad I used to be.
>
> And yet he smiles so wistfully
> Once he has crept within,
> I wonder if he hopes to see
> The man I might have been.[3]

Some regret is normal and healthy. It honestly accepts responsibility for past mistakes, which is a necessary part of wisdom. But remorse includes the feeling of guilt. Remember that it was sin that first divided Adam and Eve.

Once they sinned, something about their perception changed and their first act was to cover up and hide. Sin divided them from their God and from each other. Sin and guilt have the same effect on us. However, the mission of Christ is that of reconciliation. He took your guilt upon Himself and left you none to bear. If you are in Him, you have no room left for inappropriate remorse and no excuse for withdrawing from the Lord, your mate, or the world around you.

Don't allow yourself to become a carrier of these negative attitudes. They are a disease that will infect your family and loved ones. Fortunately, positive attitudes can be just as catching. In my own life, I can see the effect of my grandfather's attitude against that of my dad.

An Attitude of Fortitude

My grandfather seemed always younger than my father. My dad was old when I was born, and I probably made him even older as I grew up. But I never seemed to make my granddad older. He lived life on tiptoe. He found living to be an adventure—exciting, intriguing, fun. He taught me how to handle a motorboat. He took me fishing, where old men teach young men about life. And the riskiest adventure of all: he taught me to drive.

He put me behind the wheel of his '39 Ford many years

ago in El Campo, Texas. I remember ripping the front fender right off that beautiful, old car of his as I drove too fast into his garage. But my granddad never flinched. He smiled as he said, "Just back up and try it again, son. I can buy new fenders, but I can't buy a new grandson. C'mon . . . Let's try it again." That was my granddaddy. What a magnificent man! What wonderful memories! What a significant influence he had—and still has—on me!

My grandfather was like that as an old man because he was enthusiastic about life and cultivated a great attitude while he was still a young man. He faced the hardship of an aging body with an attitude of fortitude because he had learned how to face all difficulties that way. And I am very much the man I am today because of his influence. I made a conscious choice, years ago, to grow older like my granddaddy.

Again, I'm writing to everyone, not just those in their latter years. But let me say to you who are grandparents: since our young people are told to honor and respect us, let's give them a reason to do that. We can't expect respect and admiration without first earning it. If you're still in your young to middle-age years, I say, take a good, hard look at how you face difficulties now. Magnify it by ten and that's how you'll face the many challenges that accompany aging.

To everyone: look at your attitude. Like what you see? Are you weighing yourself down with feelings of uselessness, self-pity, fear, and remorse? How much fun are you to live with? Is it time for an attitude adjustment? Then what are you waiting for? Go there!

AN OLD TESTAMENT HERO WITH ATTITUDE

In my book *Fascinating Stories of Forgotten Lives*, I examined the lives of some lesser-known figures in the Bible who had something significant to teach. If I had included all of those I had wanted, the project could have turned into a multivolume set. One of those I considered was Caleb. He deserves to be revisited. I like to call Caleb "the original mountain man." You'll see why in a moment.

Caleb first appears alongside Joshua and ten other men in Numbers 13:1–2. God had just liberated the nation of Israel from slavery in Egypt and took them across the wilderness under the leadership of Moses. They camped in a deserted region called Kadesh-barnea, just to the south of the Promised Land, the land of Canaan. There the nation selected twelve men to explore the territory they were to conquer. These twelve spies were to discover what treasures and challenges the people of God would face so that an effective plan could be drawn up.

Then the LORD spoke to Moses saying, "Send out for yourself men so that they may spy out the land of Canaan, which I am going to give to the sons of Israel; you shall send a man from each of their fathers' tribes, every one a leader among them." (Numbers 13:1–2)

After nearly a month and a half, the men returned.

When they returned from spying out the land, at the end of forty days, they proceeded to come to Moses and Aaron and to all the congregation of the sons of Israel in the wilderness of Paran, at Kadesh; and they brought back word to them and to all the congregation and showed them the fruit of the land. Thus they told him, and said, "We went in to the land where you sent us; and it certainly does flow with milk and honey, and this is its fruit. *Nevertheless* . . . (Numbers 13:25–28; emphasis added)

Imagine the scene. The nation's leaders gather to hear the report. The twelve men arrive at the assembly loaded down with grapes and pomegranates and fantastic stories of how incredibly fruitful and diverse the land is. High elevations with plenty of rainfall for vineyards; wilderness for flocks; hill country for fruit trees, grains, and olives; lush valleys for crops; arid valleys for figs; a giant fresh-water lake teeming with fish; a fertile coastal plain; plenty of fresh water sources . . . nevertheless . . .

Such a powerfully destructive word in most cases. Nevertheless. Despite God's promise, despite God's demonstration of faithfulness and power, despite how unbelievably good the land is . . .

Nevertheless, the people who live in the land are strong, and the cities are fortified and very large; and moreover, we saw the descendants of Anak there. (Numbers 13:28)

The Anakim (the people of Anak) were enormous people. Their legendary size led to a common expression among the Canaanites: "Who can stand before the sons of Anak?" These were the basketball players and football linemen of their day. Imagine facing the intimidating ranks of an army of Shaquille O'Neals (340 pounds, standing seven feet, one inch tall).

If that weren't enough, these huge people built big cities with gigantic, impenetrable walls. Moreoever, there were lots of them. And in addition to these giants were the Amalekites, Jebusites, Hittites, and Amorites, each tribe tough as junkyard dogs. These were all advanced cultures with sophisticated fighting skills. Make no mistake, when looking at the challenge before them, humanly speaking, the Israelites had a lot to be concerned about.

In the midst of the objections from the majority, a forty-year-old Caleb stepped forward and silenced the crowd. I love his simple, direct recommendation: "We should by all means go up and take possession of it, for we will surely overcome it" (Numbers 13:30).

Hear the whining reply of the ten faithless spies:

But the men who had gone up with him said, "We are not able to go up against the people, for they are too strong for us." So they gave out to the sons of Israel a bad report of the land which they had spied out, saying, "The land through which we have gone, in spying it out, is a land that devours its inhabitants; and all the people whom we saw in it are men of great size. There also we saw the Nephilim (the sons of Anak are part of the Nephilim); and we became like grasshoppers in our own sight, and so we were in their sight." (Numbers 13:31–33)

I can just imagine the conversation after the meeting started to break up.

"Caleb, did you see the same thing those other ten people saw?"

"Yeah."

"Do you realize how big those guys are?"

"Yeah. But have you forgotten how big God is? Remember what He did to the Egyptians? Remember the Red Sea? God said He will *give* us this land. So why are we standing here with knees knocking, measuring enemies, and worrying over fortified cities? We have God on our side. Let's adopt an attitude of fortitude and take 'em on!"

But the men who had gone up with him said, "We are not able to go up against the people, for they are too strong for us" (Numbers 13:31). What made them shrink from the challenge? Look again at Numbers 13:33. "There also we saw the Nephilim [the giants] . . . and we became like grasshoppers *in our own sight*, and so we were in their sight" (Numbers 13:33, emphasis added). They looked at the obstacle and then looked at themselves. *Why?* Can God handle giants? Absolutely. Can God defeat a land filled with fortified cities? Of course! That's why Caleb said what he did when the whole nation started packing for Egypt.

Joshua the son of Nun and Caleb the son of Jeph-unneh, of those who had spied out the land, tore their clothes; and they spoke to all the congregation of the sons of Israel, saying, "The land which we passed through to spy out is an exceedingly good land. If the LORD is pleased with us, then He will bring us into this land and give it to us—a land which flows with milk and honey. Only do not rebel against the LORD; and do not fear the people of the land, for they will be our prey. Their protection has been removed from them, and the LORD is with us; do not fear them." (Numbers 14:6–9)

I wish the next verse read, "And so all the people took courage in the Lord their God and began preparations to receive the gift of Canaan from God's mighty hand." But it doesn't. The very next verse begins with something quite the opposite: "But all the congregation said to stone them with stones."

It's a sad fact that a positive attitude in the face of life's challenges will often be met with hostility. Equally sad, those with genuine faith in God will be in the minority most of the time.

As a result of their disobedience, God declared that the whole nation should wander in the wilderness for forty years—time enough for everyone who sided with the faithless ten to die off. However, He did promise that both Caleb and Joshua would enter the land and claim their reward.

"Give Me That Mountain!"

Now we fast-forward nearly forty-five years to Joshua 14. The new generation followed Joshua, Israel's new leader after Moses, into the land and had conquered it. The nation had destroyed the ability for the cities in Canaan to join forces and defeat Israel, but the job was far from done. Any good military strategist will tell you that the only task more difficult than conquering a territory is occupying it. The plan was to divide the Promised Land among the tribes and let each tribe overpower the enemy living on its portion and displace them.

When the time came for the tribe of Judah to claim its inheritance, Caleb stepped forward with a bold speech. As you read his words, keep in mind what he had just endured over the last four-plus decades. He was forced to suffer the same punishment as the ten unfaithful spies, even though he and the new leader, Joshua, had trusted God. While he was just as faithful as Joshua at Kadesh-barnea, Caleb faded from the public scene while Joshua became God's chosen successor to Moses. And for forty years, Caleb dug the graves of his peers, funeral by funeral, watching them die off. How many, I wonder? The number had to have been multiple thousands. Then, after forty-five years of faithfulness, he approached Joshua with the following words:

186

You know the word which the LORD spoke to Moses the man of God concerning you and me in Kadesh-barnea. I was forty years old when Moses the servant of the LORD sent me from Kadesh-barnea to spy out the land, and I brought word back to him as it was in my heart. Nevertheless my brethren who went up with me made the heart of the people melt with fear; but I *followed the LORD my God fully*. So Moses swore on that day, saying, "Surely the land on which your foot has trodden will be an inheritance to you and to your children forever, because you have *followed the LORD my God fully*." Now behold, the LORD has let me live, just as He spoke, these forty-five years, from the time that the LORD spoke this word to Moses, when Israel walked in the wilderness; and now behold, I am eighty-five years old today. I am still as strong today as I was in the day Moses sent me; as my strength was then, so my strength is now, for war and for going out and coming in. Now then, give me this hill country about which the LORD spoke on that day, for you heard on that day that Anakim were there, with great fortified cities; perhaps the LORD will be with me, and I will drive them out as the LORD has spoken. (Joshua 14:6–12; emphasis added)

You gotta love this guy. This is no selfish, gimme-what's-mine-or-else speech. There is no spirit of entitlement. He didn't expect public applause. Best of all, he wasn't asking for his retirement home; he was anticipating a new challenge! This is the same stout heart that, forty-five years earlier, said, "We should by all means go up and take possession of [the land], for we will surely overcome it." Don't assume that his enthusiasm is the result of a genetic bent toward reckless thrill seeking or that he was superhuman. A few observations of his speech will reveal some important qualities in Caleb that contributed to his attitude—qualities we can make our own.

QUALITIES THAT ADD UP TO A GREAT ATTITUDE

The first and most important of Caleb's qualities was his *unconditional devotion to the Lord*. Notice what the author says about Caleb no fewer than three times. In verses 8, 9, and 14, we see that Caleb followed the Lord God fully. I like the way one Hebrew lexicon explains the original term: "completely, formally . . . i.e., do something with an attitude or feeling of great and earnest dedication."[4] Of all the great men and women in the Bible, Caleb is the only person about which it is said "he followed the LORD God of Israel fully." The Lord was his leader, his strength, and the focus of his attention. He could ignore the foreboding dread of having to fight giants because his God habitually occupied his thoughts and clearly prompted his decisions.

A second quality was his *unwavering belief in God's promises.* In verse 6, Caleb began his speech with, "You know the word which the LORD spoke to Moses the man of God concerning you and me in Kadesh-barnea." God had promised Israel the land of Canaan, and He had promised Caleb a particular portion of it. That's all he needed for his marching orders. With those in hand, giants and fortified cities were mere details that would be dealt with in due course.

A third quality was his *authentic humility.* Given his boldness, we might think the old man was rather full of himself. Not so. Caleb was genuinely humble . . . but remember that humility is not having a poor self-image. Humility is regarding others as more important than self. Recall that back in Numbers 13, Caleb was the primary voice behind the good report. Joshua was supportive, but Caleb was the bold spokesman for taking the land and trusting the Lord. Of the two, he would have been the more likely successor to Moses—at least by our standards. But God chose Joshua.

Try to imagine that happening today. "Does Human Resources know about this decision? Joshua's a great guy, but I'm the one who stuck his neck out that day, so why does Joshua get to be the leader? I'm your man, not Joshua. Or—why can't we have coleaders?" There was none of that. During the forty years of wilderness wandering, we see a number of power struggles, we hear lots of grumbling, and we feel a growing spirit of resentment, but none of them involve this strong, natural leader. Caleb led his tribe, Judah, with quiet, contented submission to God's chosen leader, Joshua. What a remarkable team player!

And I think these three qualities, added together, gave him the fourth quality: an exuberant *attitude of enthusiasm* for taking on life. Scholars continue to debate the meaning of the Hebrew Caleb used in Joshua 14:12. Our translation reads, "Now then, give me this hill country . . ." The confusion comes because the word rendered here "hill country" is the singular word for mountain. On the other hand, the word has also been used to speak of a region or a mountain range, so "hill country" is appropriate. Some commentators suggest he only referred to Hebron, the principle mountain city. Others argue (more convincingly in my opinion) for the entire region known as the hill country.

Let me suggest another possibility. When first entering the land, the ten faithless spies were most concerned about the Anakim, the giants and their fortified cities. Remember their simpering cry? "We became like grasshoppers in our own sight, and so we were in their sight" (Numbers 13:33). Their territory was both rugged and prosperous—difficult to capture, but worth the fight. As with most challenges, great reward requires great risk. And where did these giant men with their giant cities live? You guessed it. Hebron and the surrounding hill country. Much of it being, literally, an uphill battle, this territory would be the most difficult to capture, representing Israel's greatest challenge.

I am convinced that Caleb used the word for mountain in a dual sense. "Give me this hill country. Give me this challenge. I wasn't afraid when I was forty, and I'm ready for this fight at eighty-five! God was my God then, and He's my God now. Let me at 'em!"

I love this guy! The original mountain man.

By the way, if you think he was a rickety old man, shaking his cane at the enemy while mumbling empty threats, you're wrong. He was fit because he never stopped living life. He faced forty-five years of challenges in the wilderness, which kept him vibrant and strong. And he made good on his big talk. "Caleb drove out from there the three sons of Anak: Sheshai and Ahiman and Talmai, the children of Anak. Then he went up from there against the inhabitants of Debir." (Joshua 15:14–15)

Caleb was ready to face his biggest challenges when he

was eighty-five because he didn't back down from them at forty. And my guess is that he had been like that at twenty.

ENCOURAGEMENT FOR TODAY

So what does all of this mean for us today? I've been anxious to tie all these things into our domestic world, so here goes. I want to pass on five key statements that I hope will encourage you in your marriage. These concern your mind, your life, your strength, your opportunities, and your God. Wherever you are in your marriage, I hope these will light a fire under you and help erase from your life and marriage all bad attitudes I mentioned earlier. I am convinced that these will keep your marriage vibrant and fun (even when you're still chasing each other around that assisted-living home in wheelchairs)!

Your Mind Never Gets Old, Keep Exercising It

Sure, everything on the body wears out, but almost never from using it too much. And that's especially true for the mental muscle, the brain. Find time with your mate to talk about ideas and events, and quit talking so much about people. Spend time with other "fully alive" couples whom you respect, preferably those who are a little older than you. Read more books and watch less television. Do more of what involves you actively instead of what entertains you passively. Keep developing and growing as a person. And don't forget to keep the intimacy-and-romance fires burning brightly.

Your Life Is Not Over, Keep Enjoying It

Caleb saw enough sorrow during his forty years in the wilderness, burying a whole generation of his peers, to make anyone want to lie down and die. I realize that some reading this have endured horrific pain and sorrow at the hands of a world dominated by evil. During all those dark days, it's easy to think that life will never be good again and may as well be over. As long as you have breath, you have every reason to hope for a better day. Since your life isn't over, I urge you to keep enjoying it.

All too often, though, I see healthy (and, frequently, wealthy) couples with little to complain about walking around with sour attitudes and their faces dragging the ground. I can think of no better companion throughout marriage than a well-exercised sense of humor. This is a funny world. When you and your spouse make the effort to notice, you'll see humor all around you. Here's a little story to get you started.

A man opened a new business and his best friend sent him a floral arrangement. The friend dropped in a few days later to visit his buddy and was pained to see that the flowers had a sign that read, "Rest in peace." He called the florist to complain. The florist said, "It could have been worse. Somewhere in this city is an arrangement at a cemetery that reads, 'Congratulations on your new location.'"

How do you approach life's inevitable goofs? You have a choice. A good sense of humor will help you keep difficulties in perspective and help you enjoy life even when things aren't going so well.

Here's one even funnier: Morris, an eighty-two-year-old man went to the doctor to get a physical. A few days later, the doctor saw Morris walking down the street with a gorgeous young lady on his arm. A couple of days after that, the doctor spoke to the man and said, "You're really doing great, aren't you?"

Morris replied, "Just doing what you said, Doctor. 'Get a hot mama and be cheerful.'"

The doctor said, "I didn't say that. I said, 'You got a heart murmur. Be careful.'"

Your Strength Is Not Gone, Keep Developing It

Your bones and muscles are like no man-made machine. Your body, this God-made machine, actually gets better and stronger with use. Remember Caleb's testimony? "Today I am still as strong as when Moses sent me out. I can fight and go about my daily activities with the same energy I had then" (Joshua 14:11 NET). You can bet that man didn't stay strong by spending hours lounging in his recliner, munching on chips while others took care of life.

Staying strong doesn't mean you have to be plowing fields or hauling rocks. Look for ways to help other people. Get involved in projects with your church, in your community, and with your family. Stay active! Get out of the house and work up a good sweat for thirty minutes, four or five times a week. Make it something fun or rewarding in ways beyond the physical and you'll stay at it.

Your Oppportunities Have Not Vanished, Keep Pursuing Them

I am convinced that the most crucial part of the day is how you start it. Instead of looking at the day with all of its challenges, think of the hours in front of you as a gift from God. What surprises await you? What unexpected opportunities lay waiting to be discovered? Look at this list and see if you can see something each person has in common besides his or her age.

Ignacy Paderewski, pianist and statesman, traveled the world giving concerts to benefit war victims. He was sixty-two when he started traveling and he continued to practice and give concerts until he was seventy-nine.

Golda Meir helped found the modern nation of Israel and then she served in a number of roles to keep her government alive. She became prime minister at age seventy-one, served five years in that role, and remained active in government until her death at eighty. Only after her death did the public discover that she battled leukemia for the last twelve years of her life.

George Bernard Shaw continued to write and produce plays until the very end of his ninety-four years. Few deny the genius of this Nobel prize–winning playwrite, despite having no formal education. His knowledge and appreciation of art, philosophy, music, and literature came by way of the British Museum reading room and the National Gallery of Ireland.

Benjamin Franklin became a principle architect of the United States Constitution at the age of eighty-one. Though he might be considered the last of the Renaissance men, his formal education ended when he was ten years old. Everything he learned, much like Abraham Lincoln, he discovered on his own by extensive reading.

Thomas Edison's inventions are still legendary. He continued working with his team of assistants to invent and improve technology until his death at age eighty-four. Most don't remember that his hearing began to degenerate as a young man and he was almost deaf for much—some say most—of his life.

Arturo Toscanini continued his orchestra-conducting career until he was eighty-seven. His very poor eyesight required him to conduct every symphony and every composition by cultivating a phenomenal memory.

See a trend? I am convinced that the activity and longevity of these great men and women are no accident. Each faced hardship with determination. They would not allow their difficulties to rob them of a positive mental attitude. As a result, each one was well conditioned to do great things in his or her advanced years.

As a married couple, keep pursuing fresh opportunities!

Your God Is Not Dead, Keep Seeking Him

Our Lord is timeless and ageless. He longs to meet with us, and teach us, and energize us; and He invites us to seek Him. Each day, start with Him. Through each day, stay with Him. Read and memorize His Word, believe it, and trust His promises. Trials will come for certain, but just as certain, your God will be with you.

The difficulties of life—old age being only one of them—are a question of mind over matter. I don't want to downplay the devastating effects of a tragedy. I have suffered a number of them myself as have most of my friends. But nothing lasts forever, including difficulties—unless we let them. Once the worst has passed, we have a choice. For the remarkable people in the list above, their difficulties became a platform for greatness. Their choice of attitude made all the difference.

A Challenge for You

How about you? How are you and your spouse doing in the enthusiasm department? Have you allowed circumstances and difficulties to rob your marriage of the joy it once had? Are you and your mate merely existing through time instead of living your lives to the fullest together? Don't wait for better days; you must make them better. If you don't, the end of life will come sooner than you think—in more ways than one.

My sister, Luci, introduced me to a fine short story titled *Klingsor's Last Summer,* by Hermann Hesse. Here are a few lines that serve as a warning to those who would allow life to slide by without choosing to engage it.

> Life passes like a flash of lightning
> Whose blaze barely lasts long enough to see.
> While the earth and the sky stand still forever
> How swiftly changing time flies across man's face.

O you who sit over your full cup and do not drink,
Tell me, for whom are you still waiting?[5]

I challenge you to take a different approach to your marriage, starting now. I challenge you to square off against whatever difficulties you might be facing, not with daredevil recklessness but with fresh enthusiasm and in complete dependence upon your God. Engage your mind and your strength in pursuit of a closer relationship with Him. Read your Bible *every* day. Discover His promises. Pray fervently. Seek His will alongside godly, wise, mature believers. Claim the hope He has given you in the Person of His Son, Jesus Christ.

Then, as you do this yourself, share what you are learning with your partner in life. Don't expect or wait for his or her companionship in this. He or she may not be ready. This is something you are doing as a part of your relationship with the Lord that will have a profound impact on your marriage . . . even if your spouse does nothing. Nevertheless, share with your mate how you are growing and changing as you gather strength from your walk with God. Hopefully, both of you will begin to face the mountains with an attitude of fortitude.

Where no hope is, life's a warning
That only serves to make us grieve,
When we are old!
—SAMUEL TAYLOR COLERIDGE

Notes

Chapter 1: This Is Not Your Grandfather's Family

1. Don Shewey, "The Saint, The Slut, The Sensation . . .
    Madonna," *The Advocate*, May 7, 1991, Issue 576,
    p. 49.

2. Robert Lewis, *Real Family Values: Keeping the Faith
    in an Age of Cultural Chaos* (Gresham, OR: Vision
    House, 1995), 30, 34.

3. Erwin W. Lutzer, *The Truth About Same-Sex
    Marriage: 6 Things You Need to Know About What's
    Really at Stake* (Chicago: Moody, 2004), 108–9.

Chapter 2: Getting Back on Target

1. Carle C. Zimmerman, *Family and Civilization*
    (New York: Harper & Brothers, 1947), 161.

2. Ibid., 760–61.

3. Ibid., 776–77.

4. Matthew Henry, *Matthew Henry's Commentary on the Whole Bible: Complete and Unabridged in One Volume* (Peabody: Hendrickson, 1991), 10.

5. Ibid.

6. Frank and Mary Alice Minirth, *Secrets of a Strong Marriage* (Colorado Springs, CO: Cook Communications, 2005), 122–23.

7. R. Laird Harris, Gleason L. Archer Jr., and Bruce K. Waltke, eds., *Theological Wordbook of the Old Testament*, vol. 1, (Chicago: Moody, 1980), 30.

8. Robert Hemfelt, Frank Minirth, and Paul Meier, *Love Is a Choice: Recovery for Codependent Relationships* (Nashville: Thomas Nelson, 1989), 126.

9. J. Grant Howard, *Trauma of Transparency* (Portland, OR: Multnomah, 1979), 21, 23.

10. Jeffrey Jay Niehaus, *God at Sinai: Covenant and Theophany in the Bible and Ancient Near East* (Grand Rapids, MI: 1995).

Chapter 3: Symphony of Survival in the Key of "C"

1. *Merriam-Webster's Collegiate Dictionary*, 10th ed. s.v. "dinosaur."

2. G. K. Chesterton, *Orthodoxy* (New York: Doubleday, 2001), 27–28.

Chapter 4: Practical Advice on Making a Marriage Stick

1. John R. W. Stott, *The Message of Ephesians*, The Bible Speaks Today Series (Downers Grove, IL: InterVarsity, 1979), 185.

2. Gerhard Kittel and Gerhard Friedrich, eds., *Theological Dictionary of the New Testament*, ed. and trans. Geoffrey W. Bromiley, vol. 3 (Grand Rapids, Eerdmans, 1973), vol. 3, 754.

3. Richard Selzer, MD, *Mortal Lessons: Notes in the Art of Surgery* (New York: Simon & Schuster, 1976), 45–46.

Chapter 5: Essential Glue for Every Couple to Apply

1. Jim Bishop, quoted in Bob Kelly ed., *Worth Repeating: More than 5000 Classic and Contemporary Quotes* (Grand Rapids: Kregel, 2003), 76.

2. Patrick M. Morley, *The Man in the Mirror: Solving the 24 Problems Men Face* (Brentwood, TN: Wolgemuth & Hyatt, 1989), 89–90.

3. Gerhard Kittel and Gerhard Friedrich, eds., *Theological Dictionary of the New Testament*, ed. and trans. Geoffrey W. Bromiley, vol. 1 (Grand Rapids, Eerdmans, 1973), 37.

4. Earl D. Radmacher, Ronald Barclay Allen, and H. Wayne House, *The Nelson Study Bible: New King*

James Version (Nashville: Thomas Nelson, 1997), 1933.

5. Dallas Seminary Faculty, John F. Walvoord and Roy B. Zuck, eds., *The Bible Knowledge Commentary, New Testament Edition* (Wheaton, IL: Victor, 1983), 535.

6. Kittel and Friedrich, *Theological Dictionary of the New Testament*, 483.

7. *Merriam-Webster's Collegiate Dictionary*, 10th ed., s.v. "charming."

8. Warren W. Wiersbe, *The Bible Exposition Commentary*, vol. 1, (Wheaton, IL: Victor, 1989), 611.

9. A. T. Robertson and Alfred Plummer, *A Critical and Exegetical Commentary on the First Epistle of St. Paul to the Corinthians*, The International Critical Commentary (Edinburgh: T. & T. Clark, 1914), 295.

10. C.S. Lewis, *The Four Loves* (New York: Harcourt, Brace, & World, 1960), 169.

11. Anna Quindlen, *A Short Guide to a Happy Life* (New York: Random House, 2000), 4–7.

Chapter 6: What Families Need to Thrive

1. Carlos Baker, *Hemingway: A Life Story* (New York: Charles Scribner's Sons, 1969), 31.

2. *Merriam-Webster's Collegiate Dictionary*, 10th ed., s.v. "family."

3. J.A. Simpson and E.S.C. Weiner, eds., *Oxford English Dictionary*, 2nd ed., vol. V (Oxford: Clarendon Press, 1989), s.v. "family."

4. Gerhard Kittel and Gerhard Friedrich, eds., *Theological Dictionary of the New Testament*, ed. and trans. Geoffrey W. Bromiley, vol. 3 (Grand Rapids, Eerdmans, 1973), 898.

5. Patrick Morley, *I Surrender: Submitting to Christ in the Details of Life* (New York: Wolgemuth & Hyatt, 1990), 212.

Chapter 7: Danger Signs of Marital Erosion

1. Alexander Whyte, *Bible Characters*, vol. 1, (London: Oliphants Ltd., 1959), 217.

2. William J. Petersen, *Martin Luther Had a Wife*, (Wheaton, IL: Tyndale, 1983), 59.

3. Petersen, *Martin Luther Had a Wife*, 69.

4. Ibid.

Chapter 8: Staying Young As Your Family Grows Older

1. Johann Wolfgang von Goethe, *Iphigena in Tauris: A Play in Five Acts*, trans. Charles E. Passage (New York: Frederick Unger, 1963), 24.

2. *Merriam-Webster's Collegiate Dictionary*, 10th ed., s. v. "remorse."

3. "Sometimes," by Thomas S. Jones Jr. in *The Little Book of Modern Verse: a Selection from the Work of Contemporaneous American Poets*, ed. Jessie B. Rittenhouse (New York: Houghton Mifflin, 1917), 89.

4. James Swanson, *Dictionary of Biblical Languages With Semantic Domains: Hebrew (Old Testament)*, electronic ed., (Oak Harbor: Logos Research Systems, 1997).

5. Hermann Hesse, *Klingsor's Last Summer*, trans. Richard and Clara Winston (New York: Farrar, Straus and Giroux, 1970), 166.